A BOLD STROKE FOR A WIFE

A BOLD STROKE FOR A WIFE

Susanna Centlivre

edited by Nancy Copeland

©1995 Nancy Copeland
Reprinted 1998

Canadian Cataloguing in Publication Data

Centlivre, Susanna, 1667?-1723
    A bold stroke for a wife
(Broadview literary texts)
    A play.
ISBN 1-55111-021-0

1. Copeland, Nancy Eileen, 1952-   . II. Title. III. Series.
PR. 3339.C6B64   1995   822'.5   C95-930577-7

Broadview Press Ltd., is an independent, international publishing house,
incorporated in 1985.
North America:
Post Office Box 1243, Peterborough, Ontario, Canada K9J 7H5
3576 California Road, Orchard Park, NY 14127
TEL: (705) 743-8990; FAX: (705) 743-8353;
E-MAIL: 75322.44@compuserve.com
United Kingdom:
Turpin Distribution Services Ltd., Blackhorse Rd., Letchworth,
Hertfordshire SG6 1HN
TEL: (1462) 672555; FAX: (1462) 480947; E-MAIL: turpin@rsc.org
Australia:
St. Clair Press, P.O. Box 287, Rozelle, NSW 2039
TEL: (02) 818-1942; FAX: (02) 418-1923

www.broadviewpress.com

Broadview Press gratefully acknowledges the support of the Ontario Arts
Council, and the Ministry of Canadian Heritage. We acknowledge the
financial support of the Government of Canada through the Book
Publishing Industry Development Program for our publishing activities.

Contents

Acknowledgements   6

Introduction
   Life, Career, and Reputation   7
   A Bold Stroke For A Wife   15
   Notes   32
   Bibliography   34
   A Note on the Text   39

A BOLD STROKE FOR A WIFE
   Dedication   43
   Prologue   47
   Dramatis Personae   49
   Act   I   51
   Act   II   62
   Act   III   79
   Act   IV   95
   Act   V   117
   Epilogue   140

Textual Notes   142

Appendix: Selected Documents
   A: Biography   144
   B: Criticism   148
   C: Stockjobbing   152

Acknowledgements

I would like to acknowledge the support of Eleanor Ty, Susan Bennett, and, above all, Lawrence Stern.

Introduction

Life, Career, and Reputation

Susanna Centlivre was one of the leading comic dramatists of the first part of the eighteenth century and the most prolific playwright of her time (Bowyer v). She established herself as part of a literary circle that included Farquhar, Rowe, and Steele and a number of women writers, including fellow playwrights Mary Pix and Catherine Trotter. Four of her plays had lasting success: *The Gamester* (1705), *The Busy Body* (1709), *The Wonder* (1714), and *A Bold Stroke for a Wife* (1718). The last three were consistently popular nearly to the end of the next century, making Centlivre the most successful woman playwright of the eighteenth century. Despite her prominence, however, few facts are known about her life before her first publications appeared in 1700. Even the date and place of her birth are uncertain. The most convincing evidence about her origins is provided by John Mackenzie. He discovered in Whaplode, Lincolnshire the baptismal record, dated 20 November 1669 (386),[1] for Susanna, daughter of William and Anne Freeman.

Various accounts of Centlivre's early life (some of them quite sensational) are given by her eighteenth-century biographers. The first of these was published in Giles Jacob's *The Poetical Register* (1719) while Centlivre was still alive. Jacob claimed that most of his information about living authors came directly from his subjects (Preface, n. pag.). Centlivre, according to his account (31-32), came on both sides from families that had lost their estates during the Restoration because of their support of Parliament. She was orphaned by the age of twelve and married "before the age of fifteen, to a nephew of Sir Stephen Fox" (32). She was married again a year later to an army officer named Carroll, was widowed a year and a half after that, and then married Joseph Centlivre, a yeoman of the mouth, or royal cook. Only the last marriage is documented; it took place on 23 April 1707 (Sutherland 169). Contradictions begin to emerge with an obituary by Abel Boyer, published shortly after Centlivre's death on 1 December 1723, in which he claims that she was "[f]rom a mean Parentage" and that her maiden name was Rawkins (qtd. in Sutherland 169).

Boyer also alludes to "several gay Adventures (over which we shall draw a Veil)...". The "gay adventures" form the core of the next biography, which appeared in 1747 in *A Complete List of All the English Dramatic Poets* appended to *Scanderbeg*, a play by Thomas Whincop. This collection of biographies is usually attributed to John Mottley on the basis of internal evidence (Lock 15). Although Mottley's account seems fairly reliable when he discusses Centlivre's later life, his biography is dominated by a risqué version of Centlivre's early years that features, in addition to the three marriages listed by Jacob, an early liaison with Anthony Hammond, a politician and poet. Mottley's romantic and sensational account of this part of her life made an important contribution to the growing Centlivre legend. It is also an excellent example of the way commentary on women writers in this period tended to focus on their lives rather than their works.

Mottley's lengthy account of Centlivre's affair with Hammond begins with a disclaimer: "if we may give credit to some private stories concerning her, she had for a short time a kind of university education..." (185). In Mottley's story, Centlivre leaves home when "not quite fifteen years of age" to escape "a cruel step-dame" and is discovered on the road to London by Anthony Hammond (185). Attracted by her youth and beauty, Hammond disguises her as his cousin Jack and takes her to his rooms at Cambridge where they live together several months (186). Then, claiming that their relationship has aroused suspicion, he sends her on her way to London with "a very handsome present...in gold" and a letter of introduction to "a gentlewoman of his acquaintance" (187). Thus equipped, she launches herself as an adventuress. First, she captured Mr. Fox to whom "she was married, or something like it", then Mr. Carroll who "succeeded [Fox] in her affections" until he was killed in a duel (187-88). Left alone, she turns to writing "[t]o divert her melancholy, and partly perhaps for a support..." (188). She also joins a company of strolling actors and meets Joseph Centlivre while playing Alexander the Great at Windsor (188).

This suspect account of Centlivre's early life is thoroughly gendered. It seems designed in part to answer questions about how an obscure woman could acquire the education and experience to become an important playwright. This is explained by her liaisons with a series of men: prostitution is evoked not only in her relationship with Hammond, but by the broadly hinted irregularity of her associations with Fox and Carroll. Even her unassailably respectable marriage to Centlivre is portrayed as the product of a titillating "breeches" performance. The succession of men takes her from Lincolnshire to Cambridge to London and provides her with "a kind of university education" that is continued in the capital, where she not only "learnt French, and read a great deal of poetry especially", but "studied men as well as books" (187). Finally, she becomes a writer in response to Carroll's death.

The "marriages and amours", as William Chetwood calls them (141), continue to appear in later biographies. Chetwood also includes an episode of transvestite performance although he places it immediately after Centlivre's departure from home. The question of Centlivre's education also recurs regularly. Chetwood reports that she was taught French before she was twelve by a Lincolnshire neighbour who "admired her sprightly wit and manner" (140). The anonymous female author of the biography that prefaces the 1760 edition of Centlivre's *Dramatic Works* claims that she taught herself Latin, Italian, Spanish, and French before she was fifteen ("To the World" xi). These details are as suspect as the Hammond story but they demonstrate the persistent mystery of female authorship in a time when the education of women, especially those of "mean parentage", was unusual.

Centlivre's first published writing appeared in a collection of *Familiar and Courtly Letters* in 1700 and her first play, *The Perjured Husband*, was performed at Drury Lane in late September or early October of the same year.[2] Both appeared under the name Carroll. Over the next twenty-three years, she published an additional eighteen plays as well as more letters and some poetry. As Jacob observed, "her talent is comedy" (32). All but two of her plays were comedies or farces and the exceptions were unsuccessful.

Centlivre's first play appeared only two years after Jeremy Collier's *A Short View of the Immorality and Profaneness of the English Stage* (1698). Collier's attack on the contemporary theatre was based on his conviction that it failed to achieve "[t]he business of plays" which "is to recommend virtue and discountenance vice;...to make folly and falsehood contemptible, and to bring everything that is ill under infamy, and neglect" (1). Centlivre's preface to *The Perjured Husband* refers to Collier in passing and defends her play against allegations of "loose" language.

The following year her poem "To Mr. Farquhar upon his Comedy called *A Trip to the Jubilee*" was published in a collection of letters compiled by Abel Boyer. In the poem she compliments Farquhar upon meeting Collier's challenge in *The Constant Couple* (performed 1699) by writing "language in a pleasant style:/Which, without smut, can make an audience smile" (364). In the letter to Boyer that introduces the poem, she observes that "I think the main design of comedy is to make us laugh..." (Letter XXXIX, 362). This view is the opposite of Collier's but resembles Farquhar's in his "New Preface" to *The Constant Couple* and his *Discourse on Comedy* (1702) in the value it implicitly gives to popular taste.

This approach is stressed in Centlivre's preface to *Love's Contrivance* (1703) in which, again like Farquhar, she dismisses the relevance of rules to drama on the grounds that "the town...relishes nothing so well as humor lightly tossed up with wit, and dressed with modesty and air."[3] The reference to "modesty" is, however, a concession to post-Collier morality, as is her assertion that "...I took peculiar care to dress my thoughts in such a modest style, that [the play]...might not give offence to any." Although she later endorsed Collier's view that plays should teach morality in the dedications to *The Gamester* and *The Basset Table* (both 1705), "modest" language and situations are the chief evidence of Collier's effect on her plays. Her early assertion that "the main design of comedy is to make us laugh" seems to have remained her guiding aesthetic principle.

One respect in which Centlivre had difficulty in pleasing the popular audience was her gender. After her first two plays were published with her name on them, the next five were published without it. Her eighth play, *The Platonic Lady* (1707), also appeared without her name but the dedication is a vigorous defence of female authorship addressed "[t]o all the generous encouragers of female ingenuity...." Her complaints about the situation of women playwrights resemble those of Behn, a generation earlier. Plays that are applauded while they remain anonymous are rejected when they come to be known as a woman's, she claims, and as an example she relates a story told her by Bernard Lintot, who printed *The Gamester*. A "spark" who had seen the play three or four times had bought the book, but learning it was written by a woman "put up his money" and observed "if the town had known that, it would never have run ten days." This sort of customer led Lintot to print

Love's Contrivance under "two letters of a wrong name", "R.M.", which, Centlivre complains, "was the height of injustice to me, yet...turned to account with him...". This kind of prejudice has also led men who have enjoyed her plays and knew she claimed them, to report that they were "none of mine, but given me by some gentleman...". Men are not alone in slighting her; women, who should support her, "are often backward to encourage a female pen." "[S]ince the poet is born, why not a woman as well as a man?" she asks; and cites the success of women in the arts, war, and government.

After this, all Centlivre's plays were published under her name, beginning with *The Busy Body*. Centlivre's feminism is not expressed consistently, however. In a number of her dedications, including that to *A Bold Stroke for a Wife*, the self-deprecation characteristic of the form leads her to disparage her gender. "[T]he Muses like most females, are least liberal to their own sex", she claims (x). "Women...naturally fly to the brave for protection", she writes to explain the dedication of *Marplot* (1711) to the Earl of Portland, who was also a Captain of Guards. In the same dedication she also blames women's lack of "a learned education" for her deficiencies as a writer, adding that "as our expressions are artless, our sentiments are less disguised."

On the other hand, Centlivre was unequivocal about her political views. Mottley writes of "her strict attachment to Whig principles even in the most dangerous times" and comments, "had she been a man, I dare say would have freely ventured her life in that cause" (188). Those principles are identified by H.T. Dickinson as "limited monarchy, the Protestant succession and the rule of law..." (31). These principles were also expressed in the concepts of liberty and property, which for the Whigs included the capital of merchants, manufacturers, and financiers as well as the land of the gentry (Dickinson 36). In practice, the Whigs of Centlivre's time were anti-Tory, anti-Catholic, and anti-Jacobite—that is, they opposed the supporters of the Pretender, the son of James II. They were strongly in favor of trade and, in consequence, of the military and the wars that in their view promoted and protected trade (Frushell, "Marriage" 22 n.6). Centlivre's Whiggism is linked to her feminism through the concept of liberty, which takes the concrete forms of freedom of movement and, especially, freedom of choice (Pearson 222-23). Anne Lovely, for example, speaks of the "tyranny" of her guardians in the language of political liberty (II.ii.56-58, V.i.28-30).

Centlivre's political allegiance is expressed most directly in her poetry and in some of her dedications, prologues, and epilogues. A particularly important example is her dedication of *The Wonder* to the Duke of Cambridge, the son of the Elector of Hanover and the future George II. At the time the play was published in May 1714, the Hanoverian succession was not yet secure and this dedication was a clear, and somewhat dangerous, declaration of Centlivre's fervent commitment to the Protestant succession (Lock 24). The following year she published her most overtly political play, *The Gotham Election*, a farce that shows Tories as Jacobites and equates patriotism with the Whigs. The Lord Chamberlain refused to license the play for performance; it "was objected against as a party-matter" according to Centlivre's dedication.

The dedication to *A Bold Stroke for a Wife* also has political significance. Philip Wharton, whose father Thomas had been a prominent Whig politician, endeared himself to the Whigs by his zealous defence of their government in the Irish House of Peers during 1717. They rewarded him by creating him Duke of Wharton in January 1718, although at nineteen he was not yet of age. Centlivre's dedication appeared in February; it was an opportunity for her to praise this Whig favorite and to express "loyal" Whig sentiments about his father, King George, English liberty, and the tyranny of French absolute monarchy. Ironically, Wharton had already flirted with Jacobitism when he was in France in 1716 and ten years later, when he returned to the Continent, he openly supported the Pretender.

Mottley observes that Centlivre's loyalty to the Whigs made her "some friends and many enemies" (188). Among the friends were fellow Whigs Steele and Rowe, among the enemies was Alexander Pope. The Tory, Catholic, elitist Pope had several reasons to dislike Centlivre: her Whig sympathies; her intemperate attacks on Tories and Catholics; and her class and sex, which in his view should have disqualified her from writing. He also believed, erroneously, that she had written an attack on his translation of Homer (*Dunciad Variorum* II.379n). He first satirized her in two of his three attacks on the publisher Edmund Curll, *A Full and True Account* and *A Further Account*, both published in 1716. In the second of these, she is one of the hack writers employed by Curll who are summoned to the dying printer's bedside. She is designated the *"Cook's Wife* in *Buckingham Court"* and is instructed to "bring along with her the *Similes* that were lent her for her next new play" (138). This is apparently a reference to her tragedy, *The Cruel Gift*, which was performed in December 1716 and for which, Mottley alleges, Rowe supplied at least one simile (191). Centlivre also appears in *The Dunciad*, first in Book II as one of the sleeping dunces (379), then in Book III with Eliza Haywood as one of "two slip-shod Muses" (141-145). She was also identified by George Sherburn as the original of Phoebe Clinket, the frustrated writer of tragedies in *Three Hours after Marriage* (1717), which was written by Pope, John Gay, and John Arbuthnot. Anne Finch, Countess of Winchelsea, is a more likely candidate, however, and this satire on female authorship is in any case more general than personal (see Gay 440-442).

Steele established the terms for critical praise of Centlivre in puffs for *The Busy Body*, in *Tatler*, Number 19, and *The Wonder*, in *The Lover*, Number 27. He recommends her plotting and her "incidents," elements that became the backbone of Centlivre criticism for the next two hundred years. Hazlitt, for example, writing about *The Busy Body* near the beginning of the nineteenth century, observed that "Mrs. Centlivre, in this and her other plays, could do nothing without a stratagem; but she could do everything with one" (9:79). Approximately one hundred years later, F.W. Bateson found the "effectiveness" of her plays to be "one of action and of *ensemble*, not of detail" (76). Bateson's description of Centlivre's drama as "without ...brilliance of dialogue and the sparkle of antithesis" is also a commonplace that dates from the eighteenth century. For example, *The London Chronicle* reviewer of the Drury Lane performance of *The Wonder* on 30 September 1758 admired the plot but found "the language...contemptible to the last degree" (qtd. in Agate 27). Centlivre's qualities posed a dilemma for commentators in the eighteenth and nineteenth centuries. The lack of wit and striking language in her plays meant that they were deficient in the elements that were most highly valued in comic writing, but the excellence of her plotting and the popular success of many of her comedies demanded recognition.

Her early critics explained both her strengths and her shortcomings in terms of her gender. Steele's recommendation of *The Busy Body* claims that the "plot and incidents of the play are laid with that subtlety of spirit which is peculiar to females of wit, and is very seldom well performed by those of the other sex, in whom craft in love is an act of invention, and not, as with women, the effect of nature and instinct" (*Tatler* 1:163). This view is also expressed in George Sewell's prologue to *The Cruel Gift*, which promises well-written "intrigue, and plot, and love" because these are the things in which women "take the most delight". Later critics who associate her style with her lack of education are similarly connecting her writing with her gender. For example, Bowyer quotes an article in the *General Evening Post* for 12-15 December 1772 that contrasts her achievement with that of men of genius and learning who did not produce successful plays, while she "with little genius and less education, will be remembered while we have a stage, and gain universal applause from a modest adherence to nature and probability" (183). This argument could also be used to her disadvantage, as it was in the preface to the 1791 Bell edition of *A Bold Stroke for a Wife:*

> It seems to be such a kind of work, as any woman fertile in expedient might conceive, and any woman, conversant with language in a slight degree, might write.
>
> It has no scenes of wit that demanded vivacity of intelligence to collect, and a mind skilled and exercised in remote resemblances to combine. (vii)

It was also as a woman, however, that Centlivre found her place in the English literary tradition as the successor of Aphra Behn. In her letters in the 1701 collection compiled by Boyer, she adopted Behn's literary name, Astrea, and wished "for the genius of Behn" (Letter XXXIX, 361). An article in *The Female Tatler*, Number 69, which somewhat equivocally praised *The Man's Bewitched* (1709), claimed that the circle of ladies who wrote the paper "were rejoiced to see the inimitable Mrs Behn so nearly revived in Mrs Centlivre" (140). This identification became another commonplace of Centlivre criticism, but this was not always beneficial. In *The Feminiad* (1754), John Duncombe grouped Centlivre with Behn as one of "Vice's friends and Virtue's female foes" who were "notorious for the indecency of their plays" (14,15). This is an early example of the tendency noted by Bowyer to "thrust [Centlivre] back into the Restoration" (179). The "gay adventures" attributed to Centlivre by her biographers undoubtedly contributed to her reputation as an immoral writer, as did increasingly restrictive ideas about appropriate language for drama, especially for a woman playwright. Centlivre's anonymous biographer of 1760 praised her "genteel language" ("To the World" vii), but in 1816 Hazlitt described *The Wonder* as holding "a happy medium between grossness and refinement" thanks in part to the "light and careless" *double entendre* (5:332). By the mid-nineteenth century a reviewer in *Lloyd's Weekly* objected to performances of her plays on the grounds that "her dialogue is almost always indecorous, and not unfrequently inexcusably indecent" (qtd. in Allen 262).

Despite changing ideas about the merit of her plays, Centlivre has always held a place in the history of eighteenth-century drama. In the twentieth century she has usually been recognized as one of the most important comic playwrights of the first part of the century, along with Farquhar, Cibber, and Steele. James R. Sutherland thinks that "she could fairly lay claim to being the leading comic dramatist of Queen Anne's reign" after Farquhar died in 1707 and Steele began writing essays instead of plays (168). Nancy Cotton finds Centlivre "perhaps the best comic playwright between Congreve and Fielding" (*Women Playwrights* 122) and Jacqueline Pearson argues that her best plays "are the most brilliant of her century" (228). She was certainly the most successful female playwright between 1660 and 1800. Judith Phillips Stanton's statistical analysis of plays written by women in this period shows her to have been the most successful "by number of plays both staged and published" (336). *The Busy Body*, *A Bold Stroke for a Wife*, and *The Wonder* were the three most popular plays written by a woman "by number of years produced" (333). Feminist literary history has enhanced Centlivre's prestige as the leading female dramatist after Behn. It has drawn attention to the feminism in her plays and prefaces, to her independent and sensible heroines, and to her portrayal of the oppression of women.

A Bold Stroke For A Wife

A Bold Stroke for a Wife was first performed at Lincoln's Inn Fields Theatre on 3 February 1718. It is one of Centlivre's three best and most successful plays: it was performed and remained in print throughout the eighteenth and nineteenth centuries (Bowyer 217). Like Centlivre's other long-lived plays, *The Busy Body* and *The*

Wonder, *A Bold Stroke* unites the intricate plotting of intrigue comedy, the characterization of humors comedy, and the situations of farce into a highly theatrical whole. *A Bold Stroke* also resembles Centlivre's other comedies in combining a complicated intrigue plot, which would not have been out of place in the Restoration theatre, with post-Collier "sexual ideology" (Williamson 204). The goal of Fainwell's rakish trickery is marriage, not sexual conquest; Anne's oppressors are her guardians, not a husband; and the language and situations of the play are without sexual suggestiveness.

A Bold Stroke exemplifies the kind of play that Shirley Strum Kenny terms "humane comedy," a "mode" different from both comedy of manners and sentimental comedy (29). The lack of wit which this play shares with Centlivre's others is characteristic of humane comedy, which replaces repartee with physical action (40). The play's use of disguise and its emphasis on "comedy of situation, rowdy action, and humorous characterization" are also typical of this mode (41, 42). Finally, Fainwell and Anne Lovely are the typical hero and heroine of humane comedy in the honesty and straightforwardness of their relationship, which is clearly based on love (34): they have agreed to marry before the beginning of the play and they reaffirm that intention at the first opportunity.

Specifically, Centlivre's play is an example of the humane city comedy that is the product of the willingness on the part of early-eighteenth-century playwrights to treat middle-class characters and their concerns "more thoughtfully" than did their Restoration predecessors (Corman 138). This sub-genre was well-suited to her Whig principles, which permeate *A Bold Stroke*. Anne Lovely's resentment of her guardian's "tyranny" and Fainwell's concluding statement that "'Tis liberty of choice that sweetens life..." (V.i.547) are among the few explicit statements of those principles, although Fainwell's praise for military service (V.i.537-539) and the satire directed at the dissenting Prims (Frushell, "Biographical Problems" 13) are also overtly Whiggish attitudes. Centlivre's allegiance is also seen in the profession and character of her hero; in the "identity of love and interest" in his relationship with Anne (Williamson 196); and in her sympathetic portrayal of the merchant, Freeman, and of mercantile values (Loftis 86). In addition, her political ideas are evident in the serious point that is made through the action of the play about the necessity for cooperation, not only among individuals but among the propertied interests that are represented by the guardians.

Sources

Although the dedication and the prologue claim that *A Bold Stroke* is original, it is like her other plays in being indebted to a number of sources. In addition, Mottley's biography of Centlivre claims that "[i]n this play she was assisted by Mr. Mottley, who wrote one or two entire scenes of it" (191). The discrepancy between the claims for originality and the actual synthetic nature of the play is characteristic of the tension between the "fiction" of the author's individual possession of the text, which was a fairly recent construction, and the practice of appropriation, which was still quite common, particularly in comic writing (see Munns 55). The details of Mottley's involvement must remain a matter of conjecture, but Lock has suggested that he may have helped with the scene in Jonathan's Coffee-house, since he was a clerk in the Excise Office when the play appeared (109). Lock also lists the plays that have been suggested as sources for *A Bold Stroke*: Abraham Cowley's *Cutter of Coleman Street* (1661); Dryden's and Newcastle's *Sir Martin Mar-All* (1667); Thomas Dilke's *The Lover's Luck* (1696); Cibber's *She Would and She Would Not* (1702); and Newburgh Hamilton's *The Petticoat Plotter* (performed 1712, printed 1720) (110).

The Lover's Luck bears the closest resemblance to Centlivre's play. Mrs. Purflew, "a great fortune," has two "joint-guardians": Sir Nicholas Purflew, "a formal herald and antiquary," and Alderman Whim, "a projector and humorist." Sir Nicholas is, like Periwinkle, a collector of curios and antiquities (or "virtuoso"), and Whim's speculation in patents is the precursor of Tradelove's stockjobbing. Mrs. Purflew needs the consent of both guardians if she is to marry before she comes of age; each has chosen a husband for her who pretends to share his obsession. Mrs. Purflew and her lover, Colonel Bellair, eventually outwit the guardians and are married. As Lock comments, "[i]f Centlivre did not know this play, the resemblance...is a remarkable coincidence" (110).

Sir Martin Mar-All includes two episodes that slightly resemble situations in *A Bold Stroke*: in II.ii, Sir John Swallow is falsely informed that his father has died in order to trick him out of his mistress, a device that anticipates Freeman's trick on Periwinkle; in V.i

Sir Martin pretends to be a traveler in an attempt to impress his mistress's father, an episode that Thalia Stathas connects to Fainwell's disguise in III.i (xvii).[4] *Cutter of Coleman Street, She Would and She Would Not,* and *The Petticoat Plotter* all include episodes of impersonation that resemble Fainwell's disguise as Simon Pure. In *Cutter,* Worm and Puny unsuccessfully pretend to be Jolly's long-lost brother and his servant; in *She Would,* Hypolita successfully impersonates Don Philip even when she is confronted by him (Lock 110).

The Petticoat Plotter was first suggested as a source by John Genest (2:499). Although it was originally performed at Drury Lane in 1712 and was not published until 1720, it was revived at Lincoln's Inn Fields in November 1715. This performance increases the likelihood that Centlivre would have been familiar with the play. In addition, three members of the first cast of *A Bold Stroke* also appeared in Hamilton's farce at some point: William and Christopher Bullock and George Pack.[5] In *The Petticoat Plotter,* True-love gains access to his beloved Isabella by disguising himself as the scrivener who is to draw up the documents for Isabella's marriage to Sir Simon Scrape-all. The scrivener is a Quaker named Ananias Scribe, and True-love must adopt both Quaker dress and expressions. When the real Ananias arrives, he is treated as an imposter and is about to be tossed in a blanket when he is recognized and True-love is confronted and ejected.

Cutter of Coleman Street also includes an episode in which Cutter pretends to be a Puritan in order to marry the heiress Tabitha Barebottle. Like Fainwell in his Simon Pure disguise, Cutter adopts the dress and language of a religious enthusiast. A more specific resemblance can be found in the vision that Cutter invents to persuade Tabitha that their marriage is the will of Heaven (IV.v), just as Fainwell describes his vision of Anne "growing to his side" to trick Prim out of his consent.

Quaker disguise was a common comic motif after 1680 (Maxfield 263-265). Centlivre's own *The Beau's Duel* (1702), in which the reformed prostitute Mrs. Plotwell disguises herself as a Quaker to trick the hero's father into marriage, anticipates Fainwell's deception. It is therefore difficult to identify specific sources for his disguise with certainty, although the parallels with Hamilton's and Cowley's plays seem close enough for them to be likely influences. In general, as critics have frequently noted, Centlivre draws on common comic situations rather than on specific plays.[6] She also borrows from herself as well as from others. The motif of the disguised suitor is also found in *Love at a Venture* (1706), in which Belair is Colonel Revel to one woman and Mr. Constant to another, and in *The Basset Table*, in which Ensign Lovely pretends to be a sailor in an attempt to win over Valeria's father.

Three Hours After Marriage, which was performed in January 1717, also influenced *A Bold Stroke*. There is a general resemblance between Fainwell's description of his "curiosities" in III.i and the episode in Act III of *Three Hours* in which Plotwell, who is pretending to be a virtuoso, engages Fossile in conversation about outlandish artifacts and alchemy. Both Bowyer and Stathas find that some of Fainwell's curiosities are allusions to *Three Hours*. The mummy and the crocodile refer to the disguises that Plotwell and Underplot adopt in Act V to gain access to Fossile's wife; the Dutch poet is Colley Cibber, one of the managers of Drury Lane Theatre, who played Plotwell; and the ape may be Pope (Bowyer 205; Stathas 40). Stathas also thinks that the "dame of note,/Who loved her husband in his footman's coat," who is mentioned in the epilogue, may refer to Mrs. Townley, wife to Fossile, who disguises himself as a footman to expose her affairs (100).

Structure

Out of these components Centlivre constructed a notably unified, straightforward plot that epitomizes her ability to write for theatrical effect. There is only one set of lovers and their desire to be married is clear from the beginning of the play. Fainwell has a single task—to get the guardians' consents; and a single technique—to adopt disguises that will suit the prejudices of each of them. Centlivre's skill and inventiveness are displayed in her manipulation of this basic situation through variations in the tempo and complexity of the plot, the increasing difficulty and risk for Fainwell, and the increasing suspense.[7] Fainwell adopts only a single disguise in each of Acts II and III, but in Act IV must juggle two disguises as the Dutch merchant is briefly replaced by Mr. Pillage. Fainwell's Act V disguise is the most audacious and the most dangerous. The untimely arrival of the real Simon Pure threatens to ruin Fainwell's plot just as it is reaching completion and stretches his ingenuity to the limit. Fainwell finally receives Prim's written consent at the last possible moment before he is inevitably discovered.

The emphasis on action and situation in *A Bold Stroke* is characteristic of intrigue comedy, but here it borders on farce with its "absurd and exaggerated situations, implausible complications, cheatings..." and physical comedy (Wilson 132). The improbability of the basic situation created by the terms of Mr. Lovely's will, the equal improbability of Fainwell's success, the central importance of his various disguises and the contrivances they demand from him, and the reliance of the plot on timely letters and elaborate lies all strengthen the farcical character of the play (see Stathas xx-xxi). The Act III trick on Periwinkle is pure farce thanks to Fainwell's outrageous lies and the extended business with the "magic" belt.

The play's structure also resembles that of romances and fairytales. Freeman draws attention to this similarity when he claims that Fainwell's task calls for knight-errantry. To marry Anne, Fainwell must rescue her from her jailers, whom Freeman characterizes allegorically as "avarice, impertinence, hypocrisy, and pride" (I.i.129-130). The guardians are "as opposite to each other as light and darkness" and the "quarterly rule" (I.i.81-82) of each is linked to the seasons. Like a knight who must solve a riddle to succeed in his quest, Fainwell must "reconcile contradictions" (I.i.91-92). His task reminds Betty of tales of "enchanted castles, ladies delivered from the chains of magic, giants killed, and monsters overcome..." (I.ii.45-46). These references are reinforced by the play's allusions to classical myth: Fainwell shares the god Proteus's ability to change his shape and "imitates Jove" by adopting a series of disguises to achieve his romantic goals (IV.ii.84).

Anne Lovely's situation also resembles that of a fairy-tale heroine who must be rescued from imprisonment by the hero. William Hull, in an extended examination of the fairy-tale elements in *A Bold Stroke*, points out that Anne is linked to the heroines of fairytales by her lack of a parent, her strength of character and centrality in the action despite her inability to free herself, and her emancipation through marriage to a man who will replace her father and her guardians (43-45, 47-48).

Although, as Hull argues, Anne is central to the play because of the force of her character as well as because she is Fainwell's "quarry" (45), *A Bold Stroke* is structured around Fainwell. Further, as Pearson notes, it is the most "male-centred" of Centlivre's three major plays. It has the lowest proportion of female to male roles (three to eight); women speak only one line in seven, the lowest ratio among the three plays; and women are absent from acts three and four (209, 24, n.188). *A Bold Stroke* would seem to justify Katherine Rogers's claim that Centlivre "succeeded in the theatre by writing like a man" (*Feminism* 100). Certainly, *A Bold Stroke* is the product of theatrical conditions. It owes its long performance history to the opportunity that the role of Fainwell provides for a virtuoso comic actor, who must play a total of five different characters; in addition the four guardians are excellent roles for mature character actors. But its male-centeredness is also an accurate representation of the city milieu in which the action occurs, and Anne's passivity is characteristic of the genteel middle-class woman's place within mercantile culture.

Fainwell And Mrs. Lovely

Fainwell is one of Centlivre's many soldier heroes. *The Beau's Duel*, *The Basset Table*, *The Man's Bewitched*, *The Perplexed Lovers* (1712), and *The Wonder* all have important soldier characters. Their vocation is often idealized — as it is in *A Bold Stroke* when Anne praises soldiers as women's defenders from "'the insults of rude unpolished foes,'" who ought to be preferred to men who inherit wealth and position (I.ii.54-59). These sentiments and Centlivre's choice of hero demonstrate her Whig principles, as the Whigs supported a standing army (see Butler 367-369). Nancy Cotton also links Centlivre's soldier protagonists with her characteristic emphasis on action rather than wit: the "blunt and honest" hero and his counterpart, the "forthright, sensible heroine," "waste little time in witty sparring..." (*Women Playwrights* 145).

Fainwell is also a trickster who resembles both the "extravagant rake" of Restoration comedy (Jordan) and the clever servant of farce. Indeed, Freeman warns Fainwell that his project "requires more cunning than generally attends a man of honor" (I.i.130-131). Judged by realistic standards, he is proven correct: one nineteenth-century critic labelled Fainwell "ruthless" (Ward 2:601). In the farcical atmosphere of the play, however, the deceptions are justified by the entertainment they provide and the deservingness of Fainwell's dupes.

Douglas R. Butler argues that characters such as Fainwell express Whig philosophy through their embodiment of the "middle-class" ethic, which wins them fortunes and mates through their own efforts and cleverness (370). The form that Fainwell's cleverness takes is particularly well-suited to the Whiggish capitalist milieu in which he operates. Like a tradesman who suits his manner to his customers, Fainwell adopts a character that flatters the prejudices of each of the guardians in order to get the better of them in the bargain for Anne Lovely; his success is confirmed in business-like fashion by a written contract. In this way Centlivre's soldier hero takes on some of the characteristics of that other popular Whig figure, the merchant.

Anne's position within these transactions is that of a commodity, coveted by Fainwell and traded by her guardians. Her largely passive role is characteristic of the developing position of the genteel middle-class woman within capitalism (see Todd 13-14 and R. Brown, *Society* 299-300). She is excluded from direct productive participation in the public sphere, in contrast to the repellant Mrs. Prim; instead she consumes the luxury goods provided by foreign trade (V.i.93-97; L. Brown, *Ends* 116-118). It is therefore particularly appropriate that her battle against the oppressiveness of her guardians should take the form of a struggle over her dress.

Centlivre's choice to place Anne at the Prims during the action of the play allows her to represent the guardians' "tyranny" through the particularly theatrical means of costume. Anne arrives from Sir Philip's supervision fashionably dressed in a low-cut gown with a wide hooped skirt, wearing beauty patches and curled hair. After being relentlessly badgered and insulted by Mrs. Prim, she appears at the beginning of Act V "*in Quaker's dress.*"

Plain dress was one of the "public testimonies" of conversion, designed to combat worldly pride and extravagance (Vann 188, 192). At the time Centlivre wrote her play Quaker costume was not yet codified; dress for both men and women resembled a simple version of styles current in the late seventeenth century (Frost 195; McClellan 156-157). Clothing for both men and women was to be made of plain fabrics in "sober" colors such as grays, browns, and dark greens (McClellan 225). Women were particularly careful to cover their bosoms and hair for the sake of modesty.

The frontispiece of the second edition of *A Bold Stroke*, published in 1724, shows Anne at the end of Act V as Fainwell triumphs over the guardians. She is wearing a very plain dress without a hoop. She also wears a handkerchief to cover her bosom, an apron, and a hood. Aprons, especially green aprons, and hoods were particularly associated with Quaker women, although they were usually worn only outdoors (Braithwaite 514; McClellan 140; *Spectator*, No. 631). The "pinched cap" or "coif" referred to in the play was probably a close-fitting pleated cap shaped like a baby's bonnet based on the common women's headgear of the late seventeenth century (see Cunnington and Cunnington, *Handbook...Seventeenth Century* 114 and Braithwaite 513).

Anne vigorously resists the imposition of this costume and complains: "...I must vary shapes as often as a player" (II.ii.56). As Stathas points out, however, she must overcome her distaste for deception and learn to play a role in order to gain her freedom (xxv-xxvi). Anne becomes active by participating in Fainwell's final trick and so completes the bargain she made with him: "He promised to set me free, and I, on that condition, promised to make him master of that freedom" (I.ii.42-44). Her insistence that Fainwell find a way to marry her with her money is an expression of Centlivre's "solid merchant values" (Williamson 196) and evidence of Anne's good sense: her maxim "Love makes but a slovenly figure in that house where poverty keeps the door" (I.ii.29-31) is a realistic response to the mercantile values of the world in which she lives.[8]

The Guardians

The guardians are humours characters defined by their dominant obsessions, which are displayed in their "speaking" names.[9] They are types, rather than individuals, drawn from drama and the tradition of "character" writing.[10] Contemporary "characters" provided models for Centlivre's guardians, especially those found in Richard Steele's and Joseph Addison's *The Tatler* and *The Spectator* and Edward Ward's *The London Spy* (see Stathas xviii).

The guardians represent various propertied London "interests" that divide along party lines (Lock 111). Tradelove, the exchange broker, and Prim, the hosier, belong to the "trading" interest championed by the Whigs, while Sir Philip and Periwinkle are members of the "landed" interest associated with the Tories.[11] In addition, Sir Philip and Periwinkle are "lovers and admirers of the past" and are therefore Tory in their sympathies; further, the offer of a peerage received by Sir Philip (II.i.61-63) came from the Tory party (Lock 111, 112). Despite these basic divisions, the guardians all participate in the pervasive commercial culture. Tradelove and Prim are obviously engaged in commerce but Periwinkle and Sir Philip also belong to that world, as consumers. Many of the "curiosities" that interest Periwinkle are imported trade commodities, among them hippopotamus tusks, mummies, and crocodiles. Sir Philip is an avid consumer of such luxury goods as watches and snuffboxes. In each case the guardian's foibles make him a satirical target, whether his characteristics are basically Tory or Whig.

Centlivre's satire is, on the whole, very mild. Her idea of humors comedy resembles Farquhar's in largely avoiding a "punitive" treatment of her characters (Corman 123).[12] As Corman notes in a different context, farce helps to keep the satirical "stakes...low" (114). The guardians' eccentricities are primarily meant to entertain and, for the most part, they remain unreformed at the end of the play. Instead, they are incorporated in their unchanged, humorous condition into the provisional community established by their common recognition that they have been duped. They are not "amiable" humors, however; that is, they are not treated sympathetically or indulgently (Tave 104-105). Tradelove and Prim are portrayed particularly critically, with the venal Tradelove receiving the harshest treatment.

Sir Philip Modelove is the most leniently treated, although Anne chastises him for dressing too youthfully (V.i.444-445). The beau is a common type in both comedy and character writing in the late-seventeenth and early-eighteenth centuries; however, the old beaus who appear in a number of Steele's *Spectator* papers are particularly relevant models for Sir Philip. The story of Escalus and Isabella in Number 318 is especially pertinent to the bachelor Sir Philip. Escalus is an old beau of seventy who courts the young wife of his friend until it seems she may reciprocate, when he flees. Steele attributes his "Tendency to amorous Adventure" to "the Fashion and Manners of the Court when he was in his Bloom..." (3:158).

The satire of the Prims is similar to that in numerous comedies, although Centlivre's portrayal of Quakerism is more extensive and detailed than is common in other plays (Maxfield). The language spoken by her Quakers has antecedents in parodies published in *The Tatler* and *The Spectator*, as well as in such plays as Charles Shadwell's popular *The Fair Quaker of Deal* (1710) or Charles

Knipe's farce *A City Ramble* (1715), in which George Pack, who played Prim, took the role of "Abraham, a Quaker." Fainwell's and Anne's "inspired" speech during her "conversion" in Act V is modelled on the "incantory" style of Quaker writing and preaching, which is characterized by the repetition of Biblical words and phrases (Bauman 75-77). This style is also found in parodic visions, such as the letter from "Aminadab" in *Tatler*, Number 190 that prophesies the fall of the Whig government or *Aminadab: or the Quaker's Vision* (1710), one of a series of pamphlets that formed part of the Sacheverell controversy (Stathas xviii). Prim's sexual hypocrisy is also a common feature of anti-Quaker satire which is found, for example, in *A City Ramble*. It is part of the legacy stage-Quakers received from their predecessors as satirical targets, the Puritans of Restoration comedy (Maxfield 272). Centlivre did not always lampoon Quakers—the plain-speaking Scruple in *The Gotham Election* is refreshingly frank—but the Prims are portrayed without sympathy.

Several specific dramatic examples are especially important as models for Periwinkle. The best known theatrical virtuoso is Sir Nicholas Gimcrack, who appears in Thomas Shadwell's *The Virtuoso* (1676). There is a superficial resemblance between Gimcrack and Periwinkle, but Gimcrack is an experimental scientist while Periwinkle is principally an antiquary. There is a much closer resemblance between Periwinkle and Sir Arthur Oldlove, a collector of ridiculous artifacts who appears in Thomas D'Urfey's *Madam Fickle* (1677). Fossile in *Three Hours after Marriage* and Dr. John Woodward, the collector on whom the character was based, are also Periwinkle's precursors and give Centlivre's satire some topicality (Gay 439-440). Fainwell's outlandish scientific claims in III.i are also topical; in her notes, Stathas connects a number of his lies to recent scientific research (41-42, 48).

Virtuosos were satirized because, in the eyes of their critics, they devoted themselves to trivia while ignoring truly significant cultural and ethical questions (P. Rogers, *Essays* 244). Addison expresses this view in *Tatler*, Number 216: "the mind of man, that is capable of so much higher contemplations, should not be altogether fixed upon such mean and disproportioned objects." He adds that "[o]bservations of this kind are apt to alienate us too much from the knowledge of the world..." (4:111). Virtuosos are criticized in terms that are particularly relevant to the mercantile setting of *A Bold Stroke* in *An Essay in Defence of the Female Sex* (1696). The Whiggish author compares the virtuoso to the merchant and finds the former lacking because he is unproductive: "He Trafficks to all places, and has his Correspondents in every part of the World; yet his Merchandizes serve not to promote our Luxury, nor encrease our Trade, and neither enrich the Nation, nor himself" (qtd. in Houghton 53).[13] Periwinkle is, in addition, avaricious: he is miserly except when it comes to his curiosities and he is appropriately punished when he discovers his expected legacy to be a fraud.

Tradelove is the most topical and innovative of Centlivre's targets. Although stockbrokers and jobbers, and their predecessors the "projectors," appear in comedies from the late-seventeenth through the early-eighteenth centuries,[14] the scene in Jonathan's Coffee-house is unusual in its authenticity and detail. Its dialogue was praised for its accuracy by Thomas Mortimer, the author of *Every Man his own Broker, or, a Guide to Exchange Alley* (1761) (Stathas xxii). P.G.M. Dickson uses the first part of the scene to illustrate the operation of the early eighteenth-century stock exchange (503-505). The specialized and mysterious jargon and practices of the financial market inspired both distrust and fascination (Holmes 269). *A Bold Stroke*, as Dickson points out (503), exploits the novelty of this world by taking its audience inside Jonathan's, which was a center for the market in securities.

Tradelove is described in the list of characters as "a change-broker" and Dickson argues that he is "presumably a Sworn Broker," that is, a broker registered with and, in theory, regulated by the Mayor and Aldermen of London (503, 517). Sworn Brokers were forbidden "to do business in Exchange Alley" where Jonathan's was located, "or to deal in securities on their own account" (518). Dickson describes these prohibitions as "an elaborate sham" (518), and Tradelove, of course, violates both. In practice there was little distinction between brokers, who acted for clients, and jobbers, who acted as middlemen between brokers and speculated for their own gain (Weinrib and Hibbert 848). Popular usage also conflated the two functions under the pejorative term "stockjobber."

Stockjobbers were almost universally vilified as gamblers and swindlers. Even Whig ideologues such as Steele, who enthusiastically supported trade, condemned stockjobbers as parasites (Loftis 94-95). Defoe's attack on stockjobbers in *The Anatomy of Exchange*

Alley (1719) is especially vigorous, but his accusations are typical of contemporary views and accurately describe the behavior we see in IV.i (Stathas xviii). "Stockjobbing is play...," that is, gambling, he writes;

> it is a complete system of knavery;...it is a trade founded in fraud, born of deceit, and nourished by trick, cheat, wheedle, forgeries, falsehood, and all sorts of delusions; coining false news...; whispering imaginary terrors, frights, hopes, expectations, and then preying upon the weakness of those whose imaginations they have wrought upon, whom they have either elevated or depressed. (149, 136)

Freeman exploits these practices to dupe Tradelove who in turn tries to "take in" the "Dutch merchant," first by betting against him on the truth of Freeman's news, and later by misleading him about his relationship with Anne. Tradelove's fate demonstrates the evils of speculation, which he acknowledges when he resolves not to wager again (IV.iv.16-17). His determination to reform does not prevent him from attempting to treat Anne quite literally as a commodity — an action that helps to make him the least appealing of the guardians.

Stage History And Adaptations

The first production of *A Bold Stroke for a Wife* ran for six performances between 3 and 10 February 1718 at Lincoln's Inn Fields. This was a successful run, which would have brought Centlivre income from two benefit nights (the third and the sixth), but it was not exceptional. The cast for this production was drawn mainly from actors who specialized in farce and low comedy. Three members of the Bullock family appeared in it.[15] Christopher Bullock, who played Fainwell, was co-manager of the theatre. William Bullock, Christopher's father, played Tradelove; he was a senior, well-respected comic actor who had already appeared in six Centlivre plays (Frushell in *Plays* 1:cxxxii). Jane Bullock, Christopher's wife, played Anne Lovely. She performed romantic roles in both comedy and tragedy and had previously appeared in four Centlivre plays, including *The Busy Body* in which she played Isabinda (Frushell in *Plays* 1:cxxxvii). Prim was performed by George Pack, who appeared in a total of ten Centlivre plays (Frushell in *Plays* 1:cxxxi) and was particularly famous as Marplot in both *The Busy Body* and its sequel, *Marplot*. Benjamin Griffin, who played Simon Pure, was also an important low-comic actor. William Bullock, Pack, and Griffin were the most important actors in this production; according to Edward Shuter, who first played Fainwell in 1758, "Kit" Bullock's reputation as a comic actor was established by this role (*London Stage* entry for CG 3 April 1758).

A Bold Stroke was next performed in London at Lincoln's Inn Fields on 23 April 1728 for the benefit of William Milward, who played Fainwell. After this revival, the play entered the repertory as a stock piece and appeared regularly in London throughout the eighteenth century, reaching a total of two hundred and thirty-six performances.[16] Its periods of greatest popularity were linked to specific theatres or performers. From 1729 to 1735 the play was seen almost exclusively at the theatres in Goodman's Fields that were managed by Henry Giffard; as Frushell notes, Giffard apparently had a "fondness" for Centlivre's plays (in *Plays* 1:lxii). *A Bold Stroke* was first performed at Drury Lane on 13 January 1739 with Milward as Fainwell and the prominent comic actress Catherine Clive as Anne Lovely. Clive was the most important actress to play Mrs. Lovely in the eighteenth century.

As Bowyer observes (216), the period of the play's greatest popularity began when Shuter, a famous low comedian, first performed Fainwell at Covent Garden for his benefit on 3 April 1758. At Covent Garden, Shuter dominated the performance history of the play until 19 October 1763 when Henry Woodward, newly returned from Ireland, took over the role of Fainwell and Shuter moved to Periwinkle. Woodward was a comic actor of the first rank and also a leading Harlequin in pantomime; Marplot was another role he played frequently.

The Covent Garden cast, headed by Woodward, dominated performances into the early 1770s. Between 1779 and 1786 the only performances took place at Drury Lane (Frushell in *Plays* 1:lxiii), where the versatile John Palmer played Fainwell once or twice a season. The final period of the play's eighteenth-century popularity was the result of John Bannister taking on the role of Fainwell, first at the Haymarket (beginning on 29 October 1793) and then at Drury Lane (from 19 October 1796). Bannister was a leading comic actor: he was the only Fainwell in London between his first performance of the role and the end of the century (except for two summer performances by Palmer in 1797). The Drury Lane cast also included Jane Pope as Mrs. Prim. Pope, Clive's successor as a low comedienne, was the only actress of any significance to play this role in the eighteenth century.

A Bold Stroke also received many provincial performances. Frushell records one at Epsom Walks in 1724 (in Plays 1:cxvi, n.147), and Sybil Rosenfeld, in Strolling Players and Drama in the Provinces 1660-1765, notes performances in Norwich, Ipswich, Bath, Bristol, Margate, and Canterbury. The records of performances on the Yorkshire circuit between 1766 and 1803 show A Bold Stroke in the repertory on and off between 1767 and 1801, with John Philip Kemble playing Fainwell and then Prim in 1780 and Bannister playing Fainwell 1798 and 1801 (Fitzsimmons and Macdonald). The play was also performed in Ireland, Scotland, and America during the eighteenth century (Frushell in Plays 1:lxxv-lxxvi, n.6).

Less detailed information is available for the nineteenth century but Bowyer notes that Fainwell was played by such great actors of the first half of the century as Charles Kemble, Charles Mathews, and Robert Elliston (218). The play was also performed in Australia in this century (Cotton, "Centlivre" 135). Bowyer cites an American author who referred to A Bold Stroke as a "'favorite' acting play" in 1884 (218) but an article on Centlivre in The Atlantic Monthly for June 1882 describes her as little known, suggesting that her popularity was finally waning (Huntington 764). Twentieth-century productions include a revival by The Questors Theatre, Ealing in 1954 (Norton 173) and a 1988 production by the Alabama Shakespeare Festival in Montgomery, Alabama (Gagen 40).

The production history of A Bold Stroke includes alterations of the text that reduce its length by varying amounts. However, the "added roles" that Frushell identifies in performance advertisements after 1740 were, with the exception of the "Quaker Boy," almost certainly characters that were unnamed in the original play (Frushell in Plays 1:cxviii-cxix, n. 156). "Mrs. Pickup" and the "Masked Lady" are both, presumably, the nameless woman of I.ii. "Aminadab" is Prim's anonymous servant, who is so named in the version of the play published in Elizabeth Inchbald's The British Theatre.

A Bold Stroke was reduced to a three-act afterpiece at Covent Garden during the 1788-89 season; Frushell thinks that it may have been reduced as early as 7 October 1778 at the same theatre (in *Plays* 1:cxix, n.160). These adaptations do not appear to have been published but an earlier two-act version, *The Guardians Overreached in their Own Humor; or, The Lover Metamorphosed* (1741), appeared in 1742 as one of seven "drolls" in a collection titled *The Stroller's Packet Opened*. The full title of the collection says that these farces are designed for Bartholomew and Southwark Fairs in London but, according to Leo Hughes, they also represent the provincial taste in drama (208). H.R. Falk suggests that these drolls (nearly all of which are adaptations of longer plays) were altered by William Bullock, who operated a booth at Bartholomew Fair (cited by Lock 141, n.7).

To produce *The Guardians Overreached*, *A Bold Stroke* has been substantially rewritten as well as cut. The resulting emphasis is overwhelmingly on the plot and the efficient display of the guardians' eccentricities. Periwinkle and Tradelove dominate among the guardians because the scenes in which they are duped are reduced the least; indeed, the farcical business of III.i is not only largely preserved but is embellished. Some topical references are updated: for example, Periwinkle no longer believes in Sir John Mandeville but in "Gulliver, and keeps Crusoe's steeple hat among his rarities" (127). Anne's role is much smaller than in Centlivre's play because she appears for the first time in the final scene, the equivalent of V.i. A comparison of *A Bold Stroke* with this droll demonstrates that, while it contains the basic components of a true farce, Centlivre's play, with its greater emphasis on character and satire, is unquestionably a comedy.

Another noteworthy adaptation, unacknowledged as such, appears in volume 11 of Elizabeth Inchbald's *The British Theatre* (1808). According to the title page and the cast list, this edition is based on the Drury Lane prompt book at the time that Bannister played Fainwell. Whether or not it actually represents the play as it was staged at Drury Lane, Inchbald's is a much-reduced version of Centlivre's text. For example, I.ii is eliminated, as is the episode with the masked woman at the beginning of II.i. In II.ii, Sir Philip is the only guardian to appear at Prim's, as is Tradelove at the beginning of V.i. Most of Fainwell's rarities are absent from III.i, although the business with the trap-door is intact. The "inspired" cant of V.i is also reduced. Moral considerations are evident in the removal from II.ii of the discussion of Anne's clothes and breasts,

Tobias's indiscretion, and Mary's "bubby." The overall reduction of topical and characteristic detail helps to emphasize the play's farcical elements.

The Folger Shakespeare Library collection of prompt books includes one of *A Bold Stroke*, based on an edition printed for T. Lownds and others in 1772, that is catalogued as "annotated by Samuel Phelps", the prominent nineteenth-century actor-manager. Phelps began acting in 1826, managed Sadler's Wells Theatre from 1844 to 1862, and continued to act until he retired in 1877 (Brockett 440-441). While he managed Sadler's Wells he staged many "old comedies" including *The Busy Body* and *The Wonder*, but not *A Bold Stroke* (Allen 262, 317). The prompt book is of interest nonetheless, although it is in poor condition up to II.ii. The inked-in casting shows how roles were doubled: the same actor played both Sir Philip and Simon Pure, Prim is doubled with Sackbut, and Tradelove with "Aminadab."[17] This alteration is much more lightly cut than the one published by Inchbald but it reflects some of the same principles. For example, topical references (such as those in II.i to masquerades) are cut, as are direct references to Anne's breasts. Other substantial cuts include Fainwell's explanation of the sun's cinders in II.i, the scene-setting at Jonathan's and Tradelove's stock purchases in IV.i, and much of the "visionary" language of V.i.

Not surprisingly, given such alterations, the play is generally dismissed as farce in contemporary commentary.[18] An exception is Shuter's advertisement for his first performance as Fainwell, which praises Centlivre for writing up to "the Genius of this nation" and describes *A Bold Stroke* as "a masterpiece."[19] Several nineteenth-century commentators note the importance of the actor playing Fainwell to the play's success; among these is Hazlitt, who praises Bannister's performance of the role (9:85-86).[20] Hazlitt treats the play more seriously than other critics of his time. He even manages to extract a moral from Fainwell's disguises ("*the hood does not make the monk*") and concludes "though there are many comedies more rich in wit and sentiment, there are very few more full of life and spirit..." (9:86). The moral qualities of the play were not universally recognized, however. According to Bowyer, it is condemned in *The Stage the High Road to Hell* (1767) because it encourages children to disobey their parents and mocks all religion through its satire on Quakers (217). Inchbald also found the play shockingly immoral ("Remarks" on *A Bold Stroke* 3-4), but she did not explain why; Katherine Rogers suggests that the deception of "the older generation" and the play's language may have been the reason for Inchbald's disapproval (*Meridian Anthology* xii).

In the second half of the nineteenth century the play was remembered for the Simon Pure episode, which is still commemorated in the adjective "simon-pure," meaning genuine or authentic.[21] The continuing appeal of the play is demonstrated by the London *Times* review of the Questors Theatre production. This "boisterous play", the reviewer writes, "contains for posterity an instructive string of eighteenth-century portraits" and "reveals a swift cross-section of the life of the period."

Notes

1. See Sutherland for an account of the problems associated with Centlivre's biography.

2. Information about eighteenth-century performances in London is taken from *The London Stage 1660-1800*.

3. All references to Centlivre's plays other than *A Bold Stroke for a Wife* are to the facsimiles of the first editions that appear in Richard C. Frushell's edition of *The Plays of Susanna Centlivre*. The forematter in these editions is unpaginated. Spelling and capitalization have been modernized, as they have been in the other direct quotations in this introduction.

4. Thalia Stathas's introduction and notes to her edition of *A Bold Stroke for a Wife* are cited under her name.

5. Bullock senior and Pack appeared in the cast list when the play was published in 1720; *The London Stage* conjectures that this may represent the cast for the 1712 production (entry for DL 5 June 1712). Bullock junior joined the cast for a performance on 18 July 1712. There is no record of the cast for the 1715 revival; the play was also performed at Lincoln's Inn Fields on 18 April 1718 but again the cast was not listed.

6. Lock 111; Frushell in *Plays* 1:lxix; Stathas xvii; Gagen 38.

7. The structure of the play is analyzed in detail by Stathas (xxiii-xxv) and Lock (113-116).

8. See Earle 187, 189, 197 for mercantile values and marriage.

9. These are obvious, except for Periwinkle; Stathas glosses his name from the *OED* to mean "one who surpasses or excels" (8).

10. For the changing nature of humors comedy at this time see Tave and Corman.

11. Tradelove invokes the conflict between the "trading" and the "landed" interests in V.i.xx; for another example see *Spectator*, No. 174.

12. See Corman 93-94 on Farquhar's humors and 10-11 for the distinction between "punitive" and "sympathetic" comedy.

13. For the Whig sympathies of the author, see Jones 194.

14. For example: John Wilson, *The Projectors* (1665); Thomas Shadwell, *The Volunteers, or The Stockjobbers* (1693); Dilke's *The Lover's Luck* (1696); Thomas Baker, *An Act at Oxford* (1704); [William Taverner], *The Female Advocates, or The Frantic Stockjobber* (1713).

15. Information about eighteenth-century actors is taken from *A Biographical Dictionary of Actors*.

16. The eighteenth-century performance statistics in *The London Stage* have been analyzed by Frushell in his introduction to his edition of Centlivre's plays (1:lxi-lxv). I have supplemented Frushell's analysis with details from my own examination of *The London Stage*.

17. Prim and Sackbut were also doubled in a Southwark performance on 28 September 1731.

18. See Bowyer 216-217, Dibdin 5:11, Cumberland 10:v, Inchbald, "Remarks" on *A Bold Stroke* 5.

19. *Public Advertiser* 28 March 1758, rpt. in *London Stage* entry for CG 3 April 1758.

20. See also Dibdin 5:11 and Cumberland 10:v.

21. See Ward 2:601 and Huntington 764; the first *OED* entry for the adjective is from 1869; entries for the proverbial phrase "the real Simon Pure" date from 1795.

Bibliography

Agate, James, comp. *The English Dramatic Critics, An Anthology: 1660-1932.* London: Arthur Barker, [1939?].

Allen, Shirley S. *Samuel Phelps and Sadler's Wells Theatre.* Middletown, CT: Wesleyan UP, 1971.

Aminadab, or, The Quaker's Vision. London: 1710.

Bateson, F.W. *English Comic Drama 1700-1750.* Oxford: Clarendon Press, 1929.

Bauman, Richard. *Let Your Words Be Few: Symbolic Speaking and Silence among Seventeenth-Century Quakers.* Cambridge: Cambridge UP, 1983.

A Biographical Dictionary of Actors, Actresses...and Other Stage Personnel in London, 1660-1800. Ed. Philip H. Highfill, Jr., Kalman A. Burnim, and Edward A. Langhans. 16 vols. Carbondale and Edwardsville: Southern Illinois UP, 1973-1993.

Bowyer, John. *The Celebrated Mrs. Centlivre.* Durham, NC: Duke UP, 1952.

[Boyer, Abel, comp.] *Letters of Wit, Politicks, and Morality.* London: 1701.

Braithwaite, William C. *The Second Period of Quakerism.* 2nd ed. Prepared by Henry J. Cadbury. Cambridge: Cambridge UP, 1961.

Brockett, Oscar G. *History of the Theatre.* 6th ed. Boston: Allyn and Bacon, 1991.

Brown, Laura. *Ends of Empire: Women and Ideology in Early Eighteenth-Century English Literature.* Ithaca and London: Cornell UP, 1993.

Brown, Richard. *Society and Economy in Modern Britain 1700-1850.* London and New York: Routledge, 1991.

Butler, Douglas R. "Plot and Politics in Susanna Centlivre's *A Bold Stroke for a Wife.*" *Curtain Calls: British and American Women and the Theatre, 1660-1820.* Ed. Mary Anne Schofield and Cecilia Macheski. Athens: Ohio UP, 1991. 357-370.

Castle, Terry. *Masquerade and Civilization: The Carnivalesque in Eighteenth-Century English Culture and Fiction*. Stanford: Stanford UP, 1986.

Centlivre, Susanna. *A Bold Stroke for a Wife*. As it is acted at the Theatres Royal in Drury Lane and Covent Garden. London: for T. Lownds [etc.], 1772. Prompt book annotated by Samuel Phelps. Folger Shakespeare Library.

____. *A Bold Stroke for a Wife*. London: 1791. *Bell's British Theatre*. Vol. 12. London: 1797.

____. *A Bold Stroke for a Wife*. In vol. 11 of *The British Theatre*. Ed. Elizabeth Inchbald. London: 1808.

____. *A Bold Stroke for a Wife*. Ed. Thalia Stathas. Lincoln and London: U of Nebraska P, 1968.

____. *The Plays of Susanna Centlivre*. Ed. Richard C. Frushell. 3 vols. New York and London: Garland Publishing, 1982.

Chetwood, William Rufus. "Mrs. Susanna Centlivre." *The British Theatre, Containing the Lives of the English Dramatic Poets*. Dublin: 1750.

Cibber, Colley. *She Would and She Would Not*. London: 1702.

Collier, Jeremy. *A Short View of the Immorality and Profaneness of the English Stage*. 1698. Rpt. New York and London: Garland Publishing, 1972.

Corman, Brian. *Genre and Generic Change in English Comedy 1660-1710*. Toronto, Buffalo, London: U of Toronto P, 1993.

Cotton, Nancy. "Centlivre, Susanna." *British Women Writers: A Critical Reference Guide*. Ed. Janet Todd. New York: Continuum, 1989. 134-136.

____. *Women Playwrights in England, c. 1363-1750*. Lewisburg: Bucknell UP, 1980.

Cowley, Abraham. *Cutter of Coleman Street*. Ed. Darlene Johnson Gravett. New York and London: Garland Publishing, 1987.

Cumberland, Richard. "Critique on the *Bold Stroke for a Wife*." *The British Drama*. London: 1817. 10:v-vii.

Cunnington, C. Willett and Phillis Cunnington. *Handbook of English Costume in the Eighteenth Century*. 3rd ed. Boston: Plays, Inc., 1972.

____. *Handbook of English Costume in the Seventeenth Century*. London: Faber and Faber, 1955.

Defoe, Daniel. *The Anatomy of Exchange Alley; or, A System of Stockjobbing: Proving That Scandalous Trade, As it is Now Carried On, to Be Knavish in its Private Practice, and Treason in its Public*. 1719. Rpt. in Francis, John. *Chronicles and Characters of the Stock Exchange*. Boston: 1850. 135-152.

Dibdin, Charles. *A Complete History of the Stage*. 5 vols. London: [1800].

Dickinson, H.T. "Whiggism in the Eighteenth Century." *The Whig Ascendancy: Colloquies on Hanoverian England.* Ed. John Cannon. London: Edward Arnold, 1981. 28-44.

Dickson, P.G.M. *The Financial Revolution in England: A Study in the Development of Public Credit 1688-1756.* London: Macmillan, 1967.

Dilke, Thomas. *The Lover's Luck.* London: 1696.

Dryden, John and William Cavendish, Duke of Newcastle. *Sir Martin Mar-All. Works of John Dryden.* Vol. 9. Ed. John Loftis and Vinton A. Dearing. Berkeley and Los Angeles: U of California P, 1966. 205-289, 352-375.

Duncombe, John. *The Feminiad. A Poem.* 1754. Rpt. Augustan Reprint Society No. 207. Ed. Jocelyn Harris. Los Angeles: William Andrews Clark Memorial Library, U of California P, 1981.

D'Urfey, Thomas. *Madam Fickle. Two Comedies by Thomas D'Urfey.* Ed. Jack A. Vaughn. Rutherford: Fairleigh Dickinson UP, 1976.

Earle, Peter. *The Making of the English Middle Class: Business, Society, and Family Life, 1660-1730.* London: Methuen, 1989.

The Female Tatler. Ed. Fidelis Morgan. London: Dent, 1992.

Fitzsimmons, Linda and Arthur W. McDonald, comps. *The Yorkshire Stage 1766-1803.* Metuchen, NJ: Scarecrow Press, 1989.

Frost, J. William. *The Quaker Family in Colonial Amercia.* New York: St. Martin's Press, 1973.

Frushell, Richard C. "Biographical Problems and Satisfactions in Susanna Centlivre." *Restoration and Eighteenth Century Theatre Research* 2nd ser. 7.2 (1992): 1-17.

———. "Marriage and Marrying in Susanna Centlivre's Plays." *Papers on Language and Literature* 22 (1986): 16-38.

Gagen, Jean. "Susanna Centlivre." *Dictionary of Literary Biography.* Vol. 84. *Restoration and Eighteenth-Century Dramatists. Second Series.* Ed. Paula R. Backscheider. Detroit: Gale Research, 1989. 15-41.

Gay, John, with John Arbuthnot, Alexander Pope. *Three Hours After Marriage. Dramatic Works.* Ed. John Fuller. Oxford: Clarendon Press, 1983. 1:207-263, 435-450.

Genest, John. *Some Account of the English Stage from the Restoration in 1660 to 1830.* 10 vols. London: 1832.

The Guardians over-reached in their Own Humour; or, the Lover Metamorphos'd. The Stroler's Paquet Open'd. Containing Seven Jovial Drolls or Farces, Calculated for the Meridian of Bartholomew and Southwark Fairs. London: 1742.

Hamilton, Newburgh. *The Petticoat Plotter.* London: 1720.

Hazlitt, William. *Complete Works.* Ed. P.P. Howe. 21 Vols. London and Toronto: J.M. Dent, 1930-1934.

Hellemans, Alexander and Bryan H. Bunch. *The Timetables of Science: A Chronology of the Most Important People and Events in the History of Science.* New York: Simon and Shuster, 1988.

Holmes, Geoffrey. *The Making of a Great Power: Late Stuart and Early Georgian Britain 1660-1722.* London and New York: Longman, 1993.

Houghton, Walter E. "The English Virtuoso in the Seventeenth Century." *Journal of the History of Ideas* 3 (1942): 51-73, 190-219.

Hull, William. "*A Bold Stroke for a Wife*: Centlivre's Satiric Fairy Tale." *Restoration and Eighteenth Century Theatre Research* 2nd ser. 6.1 (1991): 41-49.

Hughes, Leo. *A Century of English Farce.* Princeton: Princeton UP, 1956.

Huntington, H.A. "Mrs. Centlivre." *Atlantic Monthly.* 49 (1882): 760-764.

Jacob, Giles. *The Poetical Register: Or, the Lives and Characters of the English Dramatic Poets, with An Account of Their Writings.* London: 1719.

Jones, Vivien., ed. *Women in the Eighteenth Century: Constructions of Femininity.* London and New York: Routledge, 1990.

Jordan, Robert. "The Extravagant Rake in Restoration Comedy." *Restoration Literature: Critical Approaches.* Ed. Harold Love. London: Methuen, 1972. 69-90.

Kenny, Shirley Strum. "Humane Comedy." *Modern Philology* 75 (1977): 29-43.

[Knipe, Charles]. *The City Ramble; or, the Humours of the Compter.* London: 1715.

Lock, F.P. *Susanna Centlivre.* Boston: Twayne-G.K. Hall, 1979.

The London Stage 1660-1800. Ed. William Van Lennep, Emmet L. Avery, Arthur H. Scouten, George Winchester Stone, Jr., Charles Beecher Hogan. 5 parts. Carbondale and Edwardsville: Southern Illinois UP, 1960-1968.

Loftis, John. *Comedy and Society from Congreve to Fielding.* Stanford: Stanford UP, 1959.

Maxfield, Ezra Kempton. "The Quakers in English Stage Plays before 1800." *PMLA* 45 (1930): 256-273.

Mackenzie, John. "Susan Centlivre." *Notes and Queries* 198 (1953): 386-390.

McClellan, Elisabeth. *Historic Dress 1607 to 1800.* London: John Lane-The Bodley Head, 1906.

[Mottley, John]. "Mrs. Susanna Centlivre." "A Compleat List of All the English Dramatic Poets." Appended to Thomas Whincop's *Scanderbeg.* London: 1747. 185-192.

Munns, Jessica. "'Good, Sweet, Honey, Sugar-Candied Reader': Aphra Behn's Foreplay in Forewords." *Rereading Aphra Behn: History, Theory, and Criticism.* Ed. Heidi Hutner. Charlottesville and London: UP of Virginia, 1993. 44-62.

Norton, J.E. "Some Uncollected Authors XIV: Susanna Centlivre." *Book Collector* 6 (1957): 172-178, 280-285.

Partridge, Eric. *A Dictionary of Slang and Unconventional English.* 8th ed. Ed. Paul Beale. London: Routledge and Kegan Paul, 1984.

Pearson, Jacqueline. *The Prostituted Muse: Images of Women and Women Dramatists 1642-1737.* New York: St. Martin's Press, 1988.

Pope, Alexander. *The Dunciad Variorum. The Dunciad.* Ed. James Sutherland. Vol. 5. *The Poems of Alexander Pope.* London: Methuen, 1943. 1-245.

——. *A Full and True Account of a Horrid and Barbarous Revenge by Poison on the Body of Mr. Edmund Curll* and *A Further Account of the Most Deplorable Condition of Mr. Edmund Curll. Selected Prose of Alexander Pope.* Ed. Paul Hammond. Cambridge: Cambridge UP, 1987. 131-141.

Rev. of *A Bold Stroke for a Wife.* Questors Theatre, Ealing. *The Times* (London) 14 June 1954: 5 col.6.

Rogers, Katherine M. *Feminism in Eighteenth Century England.* Urbana: U of Illinois P, 1982.

——, ed. *The Meridian Anthology of Restoration and Eighteenth-Century Plays by Women.* New York: Meridian-Dutton Signet, 1994.

Rogers, Pat. *Essays on Pope.* Cambridge: Cambridge UP, 1993.

Rosenfeld, Sybil. *Strolling Players and Drama in the Provinces 1660-1765.* Cambridge: Cambridge UP, 1939.

Shadwell, Charles. *The Fair Quaker of Deal; or, the Humours of the Navy.* London: 1710.

Shadwell, Thomas. *The Virtuoso.* Ed. Marjorie Hope Nicolson and David Stuart Rodes. Lincoln and London: U of Nebraska P, 1966.

The Spectator. Ed. Donald F. Bond. 5 vols. Oxford: Clarendon Press, 1965.

Stanton, Judith Phillips. "'This New-Found Path Attempting': Women Dramatists in England, 1660-1800." *Curtain Calls.* Ed. Mary Anne Schofield and Cecilia Macheski. Athens: Ohio State UP, 1991. 325-354.

Steele, Richard. *The Lover,* Number 27, 27 April [1714]. *Richard Steele's Periodical Journalism 1714-16.* Ed. Rae Blanchard. Oxford: Clarendon Press, 1959. 98-101.

Sutherland, James R. "The Progress of Error: Mrs. Centlivre and the Biographers." *Review of English Studies* 18 (1942): 167-182.

The Tatler. Ed. George A. Aitken. 4 vols. London: Duckworth, 1898-1899.

Tave, Stuart. *The Amiable Humorist: A Study in the Comic Theory and Criticism of the Eighteenth and Early Nineteenth Centuries*. Chicago: U of Chicago P, 1960.

Tilley, Morris Palmer. *A Dictionary of the Proverbs in England in the Sixteenth and Seventeenth Centuries*. Ann Arbor: U of Michigan P, 1950.

Todd, Janet. *The Sign of Angelica: Women, Writing and Fiction, 1660-1800*. New York: Columbia UP, 1989.

"To the World." *The Dramatic Works of the Celebrated Mrs. Centlivre, with A New Account of her Life*. London: 1760. 1:vii-xii.

Vann, Richard T. *The Social Development of English Quakerism 1655-1755*. Cambridge, MA: Harvard UP, 1969.

Ward, Adolphus William. *A History of English Dramatic Literature*. 2 vols. London: 1875.

Ward, Edward. *The London Spy*. Ed. Arthur L. Hayward. London: Cassell and Company, 1927.

Weinrib, Ben and Christopher Hibbert, eds. *The London Encyclopedia*. 2nd ed. London: Macmillan, 1993.

Williamson, Marilyn L. *Raising Their Voices: British Women Writers 1650-1750*. Detroit: Wayne State UP, 1990.

Wilson, John Harold. *A Preface to Restoration Drama*. Boston: Houghton Mifflin, 1965.

A Note On The Text

The first edition of *A Bold Stroke for a Wife*, "*By the Author of the Busie-Body and the Gamester*," is a duodecimo printed for W. Mears, J. Browne, and F. Clay on 28 February 1718 (Norton 177). This is the only edition with authority. The copy text for this edition is the Harvard Library copy of the first edition, which I have examined on microfilm. I have collated this copy with a microfilm of the copy in the British Library and a facsimile of the Bodleian Library copy published in volume III of Richard C. Frushell's edition of Centlivre's *Plays*. The Harvard and Bodleian copies are identical; I have followed Thalia Stathas in designating these D1b in the textual notes. The British Library copy contains three press variants, one of them substantive; this is recorded in the textual notes. Again following Stathas, I have designated this copy D1a. When all three copies of the first edition agree, they are referred to as D1. Stathas's introduction should be consulted for a detailed account of the variants in D1a and a complete bibliographical account of the first edition (xi-xiii). I have also collated a microfilm of the British Library copy of the duodecimo second edition (D2), which was printed for Mears and Clay in 1724, after Centlivre's death. Although Stathas grants this edition authority, she acknowledges that it is "doubtful" that Centlivre prepared it (xii). I have adopted readings from this edition when they correct D1. I have also consulted Stathas's edition.

Spelling, capitalization, and punctuation have been silently modernized. The French has also been modernized but the "Dutch" remains as it is in the first edition. Speech prefixes have been expanded, as have contractions, when they do not affect pronunciation. Stage directions, including asides, and typography have been adjusted to conform to present-day practice; stage directions added by me are enclosed in square brackets. The spelling of Anne's name has been silently regularized: "Anne" appears somewhat more frequently than "Ann" in the first edition. The textual notes record emendations, including readings adopted from D2. In my notes to the play I have relied on *The Oxford English Dictionary* (2nd ed.), Eric Partridge's *A Dictionary of Slang* (8th ed.), *The Dictionary of National Biography*, *The Encyclopedia Britannica* (15th ed.), *The London Encyclopedia* (2nd ed.), M.P. Tilley's *A Dictionary of the Proverbs in England*, P.G.M. Dickson's *The Financial Revolution in England*, A. Hellemans and B.H. Bunch's *The Timetables of Science*, and C. Willett and Phillis Cunnington's *Handbook of English Costume in the Eighteenth Century*.

A BOLD STROKE
FOR A WIFE

Omnia vincit amor.[*]

---

[*]   *Omnia...amor.*] Love conquers all (Virgil, *Eclogues* X).

To His Grace Philip, Duke and Marquis of Wharton, &c.

My Lord,

It has ever been the custom of poets to shelter productions of
this nature under the patronage of the brightest men of their
time; and 'tis observed that the Muses always met the kindest   5
reception from persons of the greatest merit. The world will
do me justice as to the choice of my patron, but will, I fear,
blame my rash attempt in daring to address your Grace and
offer at a work too difficult for our ablest pens, *viz.* an enco-
mium on your Grace. I have no plea against such just reflec-   10
tions but the disadvantage of education and the privilege of
my sex.

If your Grace discovers a genius so surprising in this dawn
of life, what must your riper years produce? Your Grace has
already been distinguished in a most peculiar manner, being   15
the first young nobleman that ever was admitted into a
House of Peers before he reached the age of one-and-
twenty. But your Grace's judgment and eloquence soon
convinced that august assembly that the excelling gifts of nature ought not to be confined to time. We hope the example   20
which Ireland has set will shortly be followed by an English
House of Lords, and your Grace made a member of that
body to which you will be so conspicuous an ornament.

Your good sense and real love for your country taught
your Grace to persevere in the principles of your glorious   25
ancestors by adhering to the defender of our religion and
laws; and the penetrating wisdom of your Royal Master saw
you merited your honors ere[†] he conferred them. It is one of
the greatest glories of a monarch to distinguish where to be-   29

---

1 Philip...&c.] (1698-1731) second Marquis of Wharton. Created first Duke of
Wharton in January 1718, at the extraordinarily youthful age of nineteen, in
recognition of his enthusiasm for the Whig government and his father's
prominent role in supporting the Protestant succession.

17 House...one-and-twenty] Wharton took his seat in the Irish House of Peers as
the Marquis of Catherlough in August 1717. He was introduced to the House
of Lords in 1719.

27 Royal Master] George I

stow his favors; and the world must do ours justice by own- 30
ing your Grace's titles most deservedly worn.

It is with the greatest pleasure imaginable the friends of
liberty see you pursuing the steps of your noble father. Your
courteous, affable temper, free from pride and ostentation,
makes your name adored in the country and enables your 35
Grace to carry what point you please. The late Lord Wharton will be still remembered by every lover of his country,
which never felt a greater shock than what his death occa-
sioned. Their grief had been inconsolable if heaven, out of its
wonted beneficence to this favorite isle, had not transmitted 40
all his shining qualities to you and, phoenix-like, raised up
one patriot out of the ashes of another.

That your Grace has a high esteem for learning particulalry appears by the large progress you have made therein;
and your love for the Muses shows a sweetness of temper and 45
generous humanity peculiar to the greatness of your soul; for
such virtues reign not in the breast of every man of quality.

Defer no longer then, my Lord, to charm the world with
the beauty of your numbers, and show the poet as you have
done the orator; convince our unthinking Britons by what 50
vile arts France lost her liberty; and teach 'em to avoid their
own misfortunes, as well as to weep over Henry IV who (if it
were possible for him to know) would forgive the bold assas-
sin's hand for the honor of having his fall celebrated by your
Grace's pen. 55

To be distinguished by persons of your Grace's character
is not only the highest ambition, but the greatest reputation
to an author; and it is not the least of my vanities to have it

---

33 your noble father] Thomas Wharton, first Marquis of Wharton (1648-1715),
was prominent in the opposition to James II, active in the ascension of
William III, and a staunch and powerful Whig during the reigns of William
and Anne.

52 Henry IV] (1553-1610) first Bourbon king of France (1589-1610); defender
of the French Protestants during the Wars of Religion; as King, issued the
Edict of Nantes (1598), which gave a degree of toleration to Protestants in
France; assassinated by a religious fanatic who believed him to be a threat to
the Catholic Church

known to the public I had your Grace's leave to prefix your
name to this comedy.   60

I wish I were capable to clothe the following scenes in
such a dress as might be worthy to appear before your Grace
and draw your attention as much as your Grace's admirable
qualifications do that of all mankind; but the Muses, like
most females, are least liberal to their own sex.   65

All I dare say in favor of this piece is that the plot is entirely new and the incidents wholly owing to my own invention, not borrowed from our own, or translated from the
works of any foreign poet, so that they have at least the
charm of novelty to recommend 'em. If they are so lucky in   70
some leisure hour to give your Grace the least diversion,
they will answer the utmost ambition of, my Lord,

> *Your Grace's most obedient,*
> *most devoted, and*
> *most humble servant,*   75
> SUSANNA CENTLIVRE.

PROLOGUE

By a Gentleman
Spoken by Mrs. Thurmond

Tonight we come upon a bold design,
To try to please without one borrowed line;
Our plot is new, and regularly clear,
And not one single tittle from Molière;[†]
O'er buried poets we with caution tread,   5
And parish sextons leave to rob the dead.
For you, bright British fair, in hopes to charm ye,
We bring tonight a lover from the army;
You know the soldiers have the strangest arts,
Such a proportion of prevailing parts,   10
You'd think that they rode[†] post to women's hearts.
I wonder whence they draw their bold pretence;
We do not choose them sure for our defence:
That plea is both impolitic and wrong,
And only suits such dames as want a tongue.   15
Is it their eloquence and fine address?
The softness of their language? — Nothing less.
Is it their courage, that they bravely dare
To storm the sex at once? — Egad, 'tis there:
They act by us as in the rough campaign,   20
Unmindful of repulses, charge again;
They mine and countermine, resolved to win,
And, if a breach is made — they will come in.
You'll think, by what we have of soldiers said,
Our female wit was in the service bred;   25
But she is to the hardy toil a stranger,
She loves the cloth indeed, but hates the danger;

Mrs. Thurmond] Sarah Thurmond (d. 1762); a leading actress, mainly in comic
   roles
6   parish...dead] digging graves was one of the sexton's duties

Yet to this circle of the brave and gay,
She bid me for her good intentions say,
She hopes you'll not reduce her to half pay. 30
As for our play, 'tis English humor all;
Then will you let our manufacture fall?
Would you the honor of our nation raise,
Keep English credit up, and English plays.

---

28 circle...gay] fashionable men and women sitting in the boxes, the partitioned
   galleries that provided the most expensive seats in the theatre
30 half pay] since 1713, an officer could receive a reduced salary when not in
   active service

DRAMATIS PERSONÆ

MEN

Sir Philip Modelove, an old beau		*Mr. Knap*
Periwinkle, a kind of a silly virtuoso	ALL GUARDIANS TO MRS. LOVELY	*Mr. Spiller*
Tradelove, a changebroker		*Mr. Bullock, senior*†
Obadiah† Prim, a Quaker		*Mr. Pack*

Colonel Fainwell, in love with Mrs. Lovely *Mr. Christopher*† *Bullock*

Freeman, his friend, a merchant *Mr. Ogden* 10

Simon Pure, a Quaking preacher *Mr. Griffin*

Mr. Sackbut, a tavern-keeper *Mr. Hall*

WOMEN

Mrs. Lovely, a fortune of thirty thousand pound *Mrs. Bullock* 15

Mrs. Prim, wife to Prim the hosier *Mrs. Kent*

Betty, servant to Mrs. Lovely *Mrs. Robins*

Footmen, drawers, &c.

---

1 DRAMATIS PERSONÆ] for information about the actors see the introduction
5 virtuoso] a collector of antiquities and natural curiosities
6 changebroker] an exchange broker, a middleman in the exchange of bills of credit
12 Sackbut] a compound: sack, white wine imported from Spain or the Canary Islands; butt, a wine cask
16 hosier] a dealer in stockings and knitted underclothes

A BOLD STROKE

FOR A WIFE †

ACT I   [I.i]

Scene: a tavern;
Colonel Fainwell and Freeman over a bottle.

FREEMAN

> Come, Colonel, His Majesty's health. You are as melancholy
> as if you were in love; I wish some of the beauties at Bath
> ha'n't snapped your heart.

COLONEL

> Why, faith, Freeman, there is something in't; I have seen a
> lady at Bath who has kindled such a flame in me that all the   5
> waters there can't quench.

FREEMAN

> Women, like some poisonous animals, carry their antidote
> about 'em. Is she not to be had, Colonel?

COLONEL

> That's a difficult question to answer; however, I resolve to try.
> Perhaps you may be able to serve me; you merchants know   10
> one another. The lady told me herself she was under the
> charge of four persons.

FREEMAN

> Odso! 'Tis Mrs. Anne Lovely.

COLONEL

> The same; do you know her?

FREEMAN

> Know her! Aye — Faith, Colonel, your condition is more   15
> desperate than you imagine; why she is the talk and pity of
> the whole town; and it is the opinion of the learned that she
> must die a maid.

---

2 Bath] in the eighteenth century Bath, with its medicinal springs and baths,
     became a fashionable summer resort for the titled and the wealthy
3 snapped] captured suddenly or by surprise

COLONEL

Say you so? That's somewhat odd, in this charitable city. She's
a woman, I hope.   20

FREEMAN

For aught I know; but it had been as well for her had nature
made her any other part of the creation. The man which
keeps this house served her father; he is a very honest fellow
and may be of use to you; we'll send for him to take a glass
with us; he'll give you the whole history, and 'tis worth your   25
hearing.

COLONEL

But may one trust him?

FREEMAN

With your life; I have obligations enough upon him to make
him do anything; I serve him with wine. (*Knocks.*)

COLONEL

Nay, I know him pretty well myself; I once used to frequent a   30
club that was kept here.

Enter drawer.

DRAWER

Gentlemen, d'you call?

FREEMAN

Aye, send up your master.

DRAWER

Yes, sir. (*Exit.*)

COLONEL

Do you know any of this lady's guardians, Freeman?   35

FREEMAN

Yes, I know two of them very well.

COLONEL

What are they?

Enter Sackbut.

FREEMAN

Here comes one will give you an account of them all. Mr.
Sackbut, we sent[†] for you to take a glass with us. 'Tis a maxim

among the friends of the bottle, that as long as the master is in   40
company one may be sure of good wine.

SACKBUT

Sir, you shall be sure to have as good wine as you send in.
Colonel, your most humble servant; you are welcome to
town.

COLONEL

I thank you, Mr. Sackbut.   45

SACKBUT

I am as glad to see you as I should a hundred tun of French
claret custom-free. My service to you, sir. (*Drinks*.) You don't
look so merry as you used to do; are you not well, Colonel?

FREEMAN

He has got a woman in his head, landlord, can you help him?

SACKBUT

If 'tis in my power, I shan't scruple to serve my friend.   50

COLONEL

'Tis one perquisite of your calling.

SACKBUT

Aye, at t'other end of the town, where you officers use,
women are good forcers of trade; a well-customed house, a
handsome bar-keeper, with clean, obliging drawers, soon gets
the master an estate; but our citizens seldom do anything but   55
cheat within the walls. But as to the lady, Colonel; point you
at particulars, or have you a good champagne stomach? Are
you in full pay or reduced, Colonel?

COLONEL

Reduced, reduced, landlord.

FREEMAN

To the miserable condition of a lover!   60

---

46 tun] a large wine-barrel
52 t'other...town] the West End, the fashionable part of London, which Sackbut
    contrasts with the City, "within the walls" of the original city of London. As
    the financial and commercial center of London, the City was associated with
    merchants and tradesmen, termed citizens.
57 champagne] probably in two senses: an open field and a military campaign

SACKBUT

Pish! That's preferable to half pay; a woman's resolution may break before the peace; push her home, Colonel, there's no parlaying with that sex.

COLONEL

Were the lady her own mistress I have some reasons to be‐ lieve I should soon command in chief.   65

FREEMAN

You know Mrs. Lovely, Mr. Sackbut.

SACKBUT

Know her! Aye, poor Nancy; I have carried her to school many a frosty morning. Alas! If she's the woman, I pity you, Colonel. Her father, my old master, was the most whimsical, out-of-the-way tempered man I ever heard of, as you will   70 guess by his last will and testament. This was his only child: I have heard him wish her dead a thousand times.

COLONEL

Why so?

SACKBUT

He hated posterity, you must know, and wished the world were to expire with himself. He used to swear if she had been   75 a boy, he would have qualified him for the opera.

FREEMAN

'Tis a very unnatural resolution in a father.

SACKBUT

He died worth thirty thousand pounds, which he left to this daughter, provided she married with the consent of her guardians.[†] But that she might be sure never to do so, he left   80 her in the care of four men as opposite to each other as light and darkness. Each has his quarterly rule, and three months in a year she is obliged to be subject to each of their humors, and they are pretty different, I assure you. She is just come from Bath.   85

---

62 the peace] the Peace of Utrecht (1713) led to officers being reduced to half pay; it was unpopular with many Whigs, including Centlivre

67 Nancy] diminutive of Anne

76 qualified...opera] castrated him, like the *castrati* who sang male soprano roles in Italian opera

COLONEL

'Twas there I saw her.

SACKBUT

Aye, sir, the last quarter was her beau-guardian's. She appears
in all public places during his reign.

COLONEL

She visted a lady who boarded in the same house with me. I
liked her person, and found an opportunity to tell her so. She   90
replied, she had no objection to mine; but if I could not reconcile contradictions, I must not think of her, for that she was
condemned to the caprice of four persons who never yet
agreed in any one thing, and she was obliged to please them
all.   95

SACKBUT

'Tis most true, sir; I'll give you a short description of the men
and leave you to judge of the poor lady's condition. One is a
kind of a virtuoso, a silly, half-witted fellow, but positive and
surly; fond of nothing but what is antique and foreign, and
wears his clothes of the fashion of the last century; dotes   100
upon travelers and believes Sir John Mandeville more than
the Bible.

COLONEL

That must be a rare old fellow!

SACKBUT

Another is a changebroker; a fellow that will out-lie the devil
for the advantage of stock and cheat his father that got him in 105
a bargain. He is a great stickler for trade and hates everything
that wears a sword.

FREEMAN

He is a great admirer of the Dutch management and swears
they understand trade better than any nation under the sun.

SACKBUT

The third is an old beau that has May in his fancy and dress,   110
but December in his face and his heels; he admires nothing

---

90   person] appearance
101 Sir John Mandeville] (fl. 1356) the ostensible author of a collection of
    travelers' tales, who by the eighteenth century was regarded as a great liar
108 Dutch management] the Dutch provided the English with models for
    advanced trade and financial practices, including the national debt and the
    stock market

but new fashions, and those must be French; loves operas, balls, masquerades, and is always the most tawdry of the whole company on a birthday.

COLONEL

These are pretty opposite to one another, truly! And the 115 fourth, what is he, landlord?

SACKBUT

A very rigid Quaker, whose quarter begun this day. I saw Mrs. Lovely go in not above two hours ago. Sir Philip set her down. What think you now, Colonel, is not the poor lady to be pitied? 120

COLONEL

Aye, and rescued too, landlord.

FREEMAN

In my opinion, that's impossible.

COLONEL

There is nothing impossible to a lover. What would not a man attempt for a fine woman and thirty thousand pounds? Besides, my honor is at stake; I promised to deliver her — and 125 she bade me win her and take her.

SACKBUT

That's fair, faith.

FREEMAN

If it depended upon knight-errantry, I should not doubt your setting free the damsel; but to have avarice, impertinence, hypocrisy, and pride at once to deal with, requires more 130 cunning than generally attends a man of honor.

COLONEL

My fancy tells me I shall come off with glory; I resolve to try, however. Do you know all the guardians, Mr. Sackbut?

SACKBUT

Very well, sir, they all use my house.

COLONEL

And will you assist me, if occasion be? 135

SACKBUT

In everything I can, Colonel.

---

113 tawdry] gaudy, ostentatious

FREEMAN

I'll answer for him; and whatever I can serve you in, you may depend on. I know Mr. Periwinkle and Mr. Tradelove; the latter has a very great opinion of my interest abroad. I happened to have a letter from a correspondent two hours before the news arrived of the French king's death; I communicated it to him; upon which he bought up all the stock he could, and what with that and some wagers he laid, he told me, he had got to the tune of five hundred pounds; so that I am much in his good graces.   140
                                                                          145

COLONEL

I don't know but you may be of service to me, Freeman.

FREEMAN

If I can, command me, Colonel.

COLONEL

Is it not possible to find a suit of clothes ready-made at some of these sale shops, fit to rig out a beau, think you, Mr. Sackbut?   150

SACKBUT

Oh, hang 'em. No, Colonel, they keep nothing ready-made that a gentleman would be seen in. But I can fit you with a suit of clothes, if you'd make a figure. Velvet and gold brocade — they were pawned to me by a French count, who had been stripped at play and wanted money to carry him home; he promised to send for them, but I have heard nothing from him.   155

FREEMAN

He has not fed upon frogs long enough yet to recover his loss; ha, ha.

COLONEL

Ha, ha. Well, those clothes will do, Mr. Sackbut — though we must have three or four fellows in tawdry liveries; those can be procured, I hope.   160

---

141 French king's death] Louis XIV died September 1, 1715; this prevented France from carrying out plans to support the Jacobite rebellion in England and was therefore good for trade

149 sale shops] shops specializing in inferior, ready-made clothing

FREEMAN

Egad, I have a brother come from the West Indies that can match you; and, for expedition sake, you shall have his ser- vants; there's a black, a tawny-moor, and a Frenchman; they 165 don't speak one word of English, so can make no mistake.

COLONEL

Excellent. Egad, I shall look like an Indian prince. First I'll at- tack my beau-guardian; where lives he?

SACKBUT

Faith, somewhere about St. James's; though to say in what street, I cannot; but any chairman will tell you where Sir 170 Philip Modelove lives.

FREEMAN

Oh! You'll find him in the Park at eleven every day; at least I never passed through at that hour without seeing him there. But what do you intend?

COLONEL

To address him in his own way, and find what he designs to 175 do with the lady.

FREEMAN

And what then?

COLONEL

Nay, that I can't tell, but I shall take my measures accordingly.

SACKBUT

Well, 'tis a mad undertaking, in my mind; but here's to your success, Colonel. (*Drinks.*) 180

COLONEL

'Tis something out of the way, I confess; but fortune may chance to smile, and I succeed. Come, landlord, let me see those clothes. Freeman, I shall expect you'll leave word with Mr. Sackbut where one may find you upon occasion; and send my equipage of India immediately, do you hear? 185

---

165 tawny-moor] brown-skinned foreigner, originally referring to North Africans
169 St. James's] St. James's Palace, Park, and Square, a very fashionable district in the West End
170 chairman] one who carries a sedan chair
172 the Park] St. James's Park, the royal park adjacent to St. James's Palace, was a fashionable place to walk
185 equipage] retinue of servants

FREEMAN

    Immediately. (*Exit.*)

COLONEL

    Bold was the man who ventured first to sea,
    But the first venturing lovers bolder were:
    The path of love's a dark and dangerous way,
    Without a landmark, or one friendly star,   190
    And he that runs the risk, deserves the fair. (*Exit.*)

Scene: Prim's House.   [I.ii]

Enter Mrs. Lovely and her maid Betty.

BETTY

    Bless me, madam! Why do you fret and tease yourself so? This
    is giving them the advantage with a witness.

MRS. LOVELY

    Must I be condemned all my life to the preposterous humors
    of other people and pointed at by every boy in town? Oh! I
    could tear my flesh and curse the hour I was born. Is it not   5
    monstrously ridiculous that they should desire to impose
    their Quaking dress upon me at these years? When I was a
    child, no matter what they made me wear; but now—

BETTY

    I would resolve against it, madam; I'd see 'em hang'd before
    I'd put on the pinched cap again.   10

MRS. LOVELY

    Then I must never expect one moment's ease; she has rung
    such a peal in my ears already that I shan't have the right use
    of them this month. What can I do?

BETTY

    What can you not do, if you will but give your mind to it?
    Marry, madam.   15

---

7 Quaking dress] the very plain, old-fashioned, and concealing style of dress
   worn by Quaker women; see the introduction for a fuller description
10 pinched cap] pleated cap; see the introduction

MRS. LOVELY

What! And have my fortune go to build churches and hospitals?

BETTY

Why, let it go. If the Colonel loves you, as he pretends, he'll marry you without a fortune, madam; and I assure you, a Colonel's lady is no despicable thing; a Colonel's post will maintain you like a gentlewoman, madam. 20

MRS. LOVELY

So you would advise me to give up my own fortune and throw myself upon the Colonel's.

BETTY

I would advise you to make yourself easy, madam.

MRS. LOVELY

That's not the way, I am sure. No, no, girl, there are certain ingredients to be mingled with matrimony without which I may as well change for the worse as for the better. When the woman has fortune enough to make the man happy, if he has either honor or good manners, he'll make her easy. Love makes but a slovenly figure in that house where poverty keeps the door. 25

30

BETTY

And so you resolve to die a maid, do you, madam?

MRS. LOVELY

Or have it in my power to make the man I love master of my fortune.

BETTY

Then you don't like the Colonel so well as I thought you did, madam, or you would not take such a resolution. 35

MRS. LOVELY

It is because I do like him, Betty, that I take such a resolution.

BETTY

Why, do you expect, madam, the Colonel can work miracles? Is it possible for him to marry you with the consent of all your guardians? 40

MRS. LOVELY

Or he must not marry me at all, and so I told him; and he did not seem displeased with the news. He promised to set me free, and I, on that condition, promised to make him master of that freedom.

BETTY

> Well! I have read of enchanted castles, ladies delivered from   45
> the chains of magic, giants killed, and monsters overcome; so
> that I shall be the less surprised if the Colonel should conjure
> you out of the power of your guardians. If he does, I am sure
> he deserves your fortune.

MRS. LOVELY

> And shall have it, girl, if it were ten times as much. For I'll in-   50
> genuously confess to thee, that I do like the Colonel above all
> men I ever saw. There's something so *gentil* in a soldier, a kind
> of *je ne sais quoi* air that makes 'em more agreeable than the
> rest of mankind. They command regard, as who should say,
> "we are your defenders, we preserve your beauties from the   55
> insults of rude, unpolished foes," and ought to be preferred
> before those lazy, indolent mortals, who, by dropping into
> their father's estate, set up their coaches and think to rattle
> themselves into our affections.

BETTY

> Nay, madam, I confess that the army has engrossed all the   60
> prettiest fellows. A laced coat and feather have irresistible
> charms.

MRS. LOVELY

> But the Colonel has all the beauties of the mind, as well as
> person. Oh all ye powers that favor happy lovers, grant he
> may be mine! Thou god of love, if thou be'st ought but name,   65
> assist my Fainwell.
> Point all thy darts to aid my love's design,
> And make his plots as prevalent as thine.†

---

52 *gentil*] well-bred, genteel
53 *je...quoi*] I don't know what; an indescribable something

ACT II

Scene: the Park.

Enter Colonel finely dressed, three footmen after him.

COLONEL

So, now if I can but meet this beau. Egad, methinks I cut a
smart figure, and have as much of the tawdry air as any Italian
count or French marquis of 'em all. Sure I shall know this
knight again. — Ha! Yonder he sits, making love to a mask,
i'faith. I'll walk up the Mall, and come down by him. (*Exit.*)   5

> *Scene draws and discovers Sir Philip*
> *upon a bench with a woman, masked.*

SIR PHILIP

Well, but, my dear, are you really constant to your keeper?

WOMAN

Yes, really, sir. Hey day! Who comes yonder? He cuts a
mighty figure.

SIR PHILIP

Ha! A stranger, by his equipage keeping so close at his heels.
He has the appearance of a man of quality. Positively, French   10
by his dancing air.

WOMAN

He crosses, as if he meant to sit down here.

SIR PHILIP

He has a mind to make love to thee, child.

> *Enter Colonel and seats himself*
> *upon the bench by Sir Philip.*

---

4 making...mask] courting a woman wearing a mask; by this time, masks were
   associated with prostitutes, for which St. James's Park was notorious
5 the Mall] fashionable promenade forming the northern boundary of St. James's
   Park
SD: *Scene draws*] shutters (flat wings that meet at center stage) slide off stage in
   grooves to reveal ("discover") a setting or tableau

WOMAN

It will be to no purpose if he does.

SIR PHILIP

Are you resolved to be cruel then?   15

COLONEL

You must be very cruel, indeed, if you can deny anything to
so fine a gentleman, madam. (*Takes out his watch.*)

WOMAN

I never mind the outside of a man.

COLONEL

And I'm afraid thou art no judge of the inside.

SIR PHILIP

I am, positively, of your mind, sir. For creatures of her func-   20
tion seldom penetrate beyond the pocket.

WOMAN

(*Aside.*) Creatures of your composition have, indeed, generally more in their pockets than in their heads.

SIR PHILIP

Pray what says your watch? Mine is down. (*Pulling out his
watch.*)   25

COLONEL

I want thirty-six minutes of twelve, sir. (*Puts up his watch and
takes out his snuffbox.*)

SIR PHILIP

May I presume, sir?

COLONEL

Sir, you honor me. (*Presenting the box.*)

SIR PHILIP

[*Aside.*] He speaks good English, though he must be a for-   30
eigner. [*To him.*] This snuff is extremely good and the box
prodigious fine; the work is French I presume, sir.

COLONEL

I bought it in Paris, sir. I do think the workmanship pretty
neat.

SIR PHILIP

Neat, 'tis exquisitely fine, sir; pray, sir, if I may take the liberty   35
of inquiring — what country is so happy to claim the birth
of the finest gentleman in the universe? France, I presume.

COLONEL

Then you don't think me an Englishman?

SIR PHILIP
> No, upon my soul don't I.

COLONEL
> I am sorry for't.   40

SIR PHILIP
> Impossible you should wish to be an Englishman. Pardon me, sir, this island could not produce a person of such alertness.

COLONEL
> As this mirror shows you, Sir. (*Puts up a pocket-glass to Sir Philip's face.*)

WOMAN
> [*Aside.*] Coxcombs,[†] I'm sick to hear 'em praise one another;   45
> one seldom gets anything by such animals, not even a dinner, unless one can dine upon soup and celery. (*Exit.*)

SIR PHILIP
> Oh Ged, Sir! Will you leave us, madam? Ha, ha.

COLONEL
> She fears 'twill be only losing time to stay here, ha, ha. I know not how to distinguish you, sir, but your mien and address   50
> speak you Right Honorable.

SIR PHILIP
> Thus great souls judge of others by themselves. I am only adorned with knighthood, that's all I assure you, sir; my name is Sir Philip Modelove.

COLONEL
> Of French extraction?   55

SIR PHILIP
> My father was French.

COLONEL
> One may plainly perceive it — there is a certain gaiety peculiar to my nation (for I will own myself a Frenchman), which distinguishes us everywhere. A person of your figure would be a vast addition to a coronet.   60

---

45 Coxcombs] foolish, conceited people, vain of their appearance or dress; fops
47 soup and celery] meagre French cuisine
51 Right Honorable] i.e. a member of the nobility

SIR PHILIP

    I must own, I had the offer of a barony about five years ago,
but I abhorred the fatigue which must have attended it. I
could never yet bring myself to join with either party.

COLONEL

    You are perfectly in the right, Sir Philip. A fine person should
not embark himself in the slovenly concern of politics; dress   65
and pleasure are objects proper for the soul of a fine gentleman.

SIR PHILIP

    And love —

COLONEL

    Oh! That's included under the article of pleasure.

SIR PHILIP

    Parbleu, il est un homme d'esprit, I must embrace you. (*Rises and*   70
embraces.) Your sentiments are so agreeable to mine that we
appear to have but one soul, for our ideas and conceptions are
the same.

COLONEL

    (*Aside.*) I should be sorry for that. [*To him.*] You do me too
much honor, Sir Philip.   75

SIR PHILIP

    Your vivacity and[†] *gentil* mien assured me at first sight there
was nothing of this foggy island in your composition. May I
crave your name, sir?

COLONEL

    My name is La Fainwell, sir, at your service.

SIR PHILIP

    The La Fainwells are French, I know; though the name is be-   80
come very numerous in Great Britain of late years. I was sure
you was French the moment I laid my eyes upon you; I could
not come into the supposition of your being an Englishman;
this island produces few such ornaments.

COLONEL

    Pardon me, Sir Philip, this island has two things superior to all   85
nations under the sun.

---

61 offer...ago] a reference to Queen Anne's creation of twelve new Tory peers in
   1712 to ensure that the Treaty of Utrecht would pass the House of Lords
70 *Parbleu...d'esprit*] By Jove, he is a man of wit

SIR PHILIP

Aye! What are they?

COLONEL

The ladies and the laws.

SIR PHILIP

The laws indeed do claim a preference of other nations, but
by my soul there are fine women everywhere. I must own I   90
have felt their power in all countries.

COLONEL

There are some finished beauties, I confess, in France, Italy,
Germany, nay, even in Holland; *mais sont bien rares.* But *les
belles anglaises!* Oh, Sir Philip, where find we such women!
Such symmetry of shape! Such elegancy of dress! Such regu-   95
larity of features! Such sweetness of temper! Such command-
ing eyes! And such bewitching smiles?

SIR PHILIP

Ah! *Parbleu vous êtes attraper.*

COLONEL

Non, je vous assure, chevalier — but I declare there is no amuse-
ment so agreeable to my *goût,* as the conversation of a fine   100
woman. I could never be prevailed upon to enter into what
the vulgar calls the pleasure of the bottle.

SIR PHILIP

My own taste, *positivement.* A ball or a masquerade is certainly
preferable to all the productions of the vineyard.

COLONEL

Infinitely! I hope the people of quality in England will sup-   105
port that branch of pleasure which was imported with their
peace and since naturalized by the ingenious Mr. Heidegger.

---

93 *mais...rares*] but they are very rare
93-4 *les...anglaises*] the English beauties
98 *Parbleu...attraper.*] By Jove, you have been taken in.
99 *Non...chevalier*] No, I assure you, knight
100 *goût*] taste
103 *positivement*] positively
106-7 branch...peace] the French ambassador to England, the Duc D'Aumont,
    held some of the earliest masked balls in London in 1713, after the Peace of
    Utrecht (Castle 9)
107 Mr. Heidegger] John James ("Count") Heidegger (1659?-1749), the manager
    of the Haymarket Theater, who began presenting public masquerades there in
    1717

SIR PHILIP

> The ladies assure me it will become part of the constitution, upon which I subscribed an hundred guineas. It will be of great service to the public, at least to the Company of Sur- 110 geons and the City in general.

COLONEL

> Ha, ha, it may help to ennoble the blood of the City. Are you married, Sir Philip?

SIR PHILIP

> No, nor do I believe I ever shall enter into that honorable state; I have an absolute tender for the whole sex. 115

COLONEL

> (*Aside.*) That's more than they have for you I dare swear.

SIR PHILIP

> And I have the honor to be very well with the ladies, I can assure you, sir, and I won't affront a million of fine women to make one happy.

COLONEL

> Nay, marriage is really reducing a man's taste to a kind of 120 half-pleasure, but then it carries the blessing of peace along with it; one goes to sleep without fear and wakes without pain.

SIR PHILIP

> There is something of that in't; a wife is a very good dish for an English stomach, but gross feeding for nicer palates, ha, ha, 125 ha!

110-11 Company of Surgeons] the doctors' guild, the members of which will be paid for cures for venereal disease

112 ennoble...City] masquerades were condemned for promoting immorality and the indiscriminate mingling of classes

115 tender for] fondness for

COLONEL

> I find I was very much mistaken — I imagined you had been
> married to that young lady which I saw in the chariot with
> you this morning in Gracechurch Street.

SIR PHILIP

> Who, Nancy Lovely? I am a piece of a guardian to that lady,   130
> you must know; her father, I thank him, joined me with three
> of the most preposterous old fellows — that upon my soul
> I'm in pain for the poor girl — she must certainly lead apes,
> as the saying is; ha, ha.

COLONEL

> That's pity. Sir Philip, if the lady would give me leave, I would   135
> endeavor to avert that curse.

SIR PHILIP

> As to the lady, she'd gladly be rid of us at any rate, I believe;
> but here's the mischief, he who marries Miss Lovely, must
> have the consent of us all four, or not a penny of her portion.
> For my part, I shall never approve of any but a man of figure,   140
> and the rest are not only averse to cleanliness, but have each a
> peculiar taste to gratify. For my part, I declare, I would prefer
> you to all men I ever saw —

COLONEL

> And I her to all women —

SIR PHILIP

> I assure you, Mr. Fainwell, I am for marrying her, for I hate   145
> the trouble of a guardian, especially among such wretches;
> but resolve never to agree to the choice of any one of them,
> and I fancy they'll be even with me, for they never came into
> any proposal of mine yet.

COLONEL

> I wish I had your leave to try them, Sir Philip.   150

SIR PHILIP

> With all my soul, sir, I can refuse a person of your appearance
> nothing.

---

128 chariot] a light four-wheeled carriage with only back seats

129 Gracechurch Street] in the City, running from London Bridge and the
Monument to Cornhill; nearby was the oldest Quaker meeting-house in
London

133 lead apes] proverbial: old maids lead apes in hell as punishment for not
marrying while they could

COLONEL

    Sir, I am infinitely obliged to you.

SIR PHILIP

    But do you really like matrimony?

COLONEL

    I believe I could with that lady, sir.   155

SIR PHILIP

    The only point in which we differ — but you are master of
so many qualifications that I can excuse one fault, for I must
think it a fault in a fine gentleman; and that you are such, I'll
give it under my hand.

COLONEL

    I wish you'd give me your consent to marry Mrs. Lovely un-   160
der your hand, Sir Philip.

SIR PHILIP

    I'll do't, if you'll step into St. James's Coffee-house, where we
may have pen and ink. Though I can't forsee what advantage
my consent will be to you without you could find a way to
get the rest of the guardians'. But I'll introduce you, however;   165
she is now at a Quaker's where I carried her this morning,
when you saw us in Gracechurch Street. I assure you she has
an odd *ragoût* of guardians, as you will find when you hear the
characters, which I'll endeavor to give you as we go along. —
Hey! Pierre, Jacques, Renault — where are you all, scoun-   170
drels? Order the chariot to St. James's Coffee-house.

COLONEL

    Le noir, le brun, le blanc — *mortbleu, où sont ces coquins-là? Allons,
monsieur le chevalier.*

SIR PHILIP

    Ah! *Pardonnez moi, monsieur.*

COLONEL

    Not one step, upon my soul, Sir Philip.   175

---

162 St. James's Coffee-house] 87 St. James's Street; a Whig establishment,
    patronized by Steele and Addison and associated with *The Tatler*

168 *ragoût*] stew; fig. mixture

172 *Le noir...chevalier.*] The black, the brown, the white — zounds, where are
    these rascals? Let us go, sir knight.

174 *Pardonnez...monsieur.*] Excuse me, sir. Each tries to get the other to go first.

SIR PHILIP

The best-bred man in Europe, positively.

Exeunt.

Scene changes to Obadiah Prim's house. [II.i

Enter Mrs. Lovely followed by Mrs. Prim.

MRS PRIM

Then thou wilt not obey me; and thou dost really think those fallals becometh thee?

MRS. LOVELY

I do, indeed.

MRS. PRIM

Now will I be judged by all sober people, if I don't look more like a modest woman than thou dost, Anne. 5

MRS. LOVELY

More like a hypocrite, you mean, Mrs. Prim.

MRS. PRIM

Ah! Anne, Anne, that wicked Philip Modelove will undo thee. Satan so fills thy heart with pride during the three months of his guardianship, that thou becomest a stumbling-block to the upright. 10

MRS. LOVELY

Pray, who are they? Are the pinched cap and formal hood the emblems of sanctity? Does your virtue consist in your dress, Mrs. Prim?

---

1 thou] the use of "thee" and "thou" was one of the Quaker "public testimonies" of conversion; it was intended to reproduce Biblical language and to eliminate one of the designations of rank, since inferiors were expected to use "you" to their superiors

2 fallals] showy decorations of dress

11 formal] conventional, with the implication of form without substance

11 hood] soft, concealing hood worn by women; associated with Quaker women, who wore hoods for the sake of modesty whenever they left their houses

MRS. PRIM

It doth not consist in cut hair, spotted face, and bare necks.
Oh, the wickedness of this generation! The primitive women   15
knew not the abomination of hooped petticoats.

MRS. LOVELY

No, nor the abomination of cant neither. Don't tell me, Mrs.
Prim, don't. I know you have as much pride, vanity, self-con-
ceit, and ambition among you, couched under that formal
habit and sanctified countenance, as the proudest of us all; but   20
the world begins to see your prudery.†

MRS. PRIM

Prudery!† What! Do they invent new words as well as new
fashions? Ah! Poor, fantastic age, I pity thee. Poor deluded
Anne, which dost thou think most resemblest the saint and
which the sinner, thy dress or mine? Thy naked bosom al-   25
lureth the eye of the bystander, encourageth the frailty of hu-
man nature, and corrupteth the soul with evil longings.

MRS. LOVELY

And pray who corrupted your son Tobias with evil longings?
Your maid Tabitha wore a handkerchief, and yet he made the
saint a sinner.   30

MRS. PRIM

Well, well, spit thy malice. I confess Satan did buffet my son
Tobias and my servant Tabitha; the evil spirit was at that time
too strong and they both became subject to its workings —
not from any outward provocation — but from an inward
call; he was not tainted with the rottenness of the fashions,   35
nor did his eyes take in the drunkeness of beauty.

---

14 cut hair] hair trimmed to frame the face, rather than being pulled straight back
14 spotted face] fashionably decorated with patches made of silk or velvet
15 primitive women] women of the earliest Christian church
16 hooped petticoats] large hoops worn under skirts
20 habit] clothing
22 Prudery...new words] prudishness; originally a French word; the first recorded
   English usage occurs in *The Tatler*, No. 126 (1709)
29 handkerchief] a large square of fine cloth folded and draped around the neck to
   conceal a low neckline
30 saint] a person making an outward show of piety; pejoratively applied to
   Dissenters

MRS. LOVELY

No! That's plainly to be seen.

MRS. PRIM

Tabitha is one of the faithful, he fell not with a stranger.

MRS. LOVELY

So! Then you hold wenching no crime, provided it be within
the pale of your own tribe. You are an excellent casuist, truly.   40

Enter Obadiah Prim.

OBADIAH PRIM

Not stripped of thy vanity yet, Anne? Why dost not thou
make her put it off, Sarah?

MRS. PRIM

She will not do it.

OBADIAH PRIM

Verily, thy naked breasts troubleth my outward man; I pray
thee hide 'em, Anne; put on a handkerchief, Anne Lovely.   45

MRS. LOVELY

I hate handkerchiefs when 'tis not cold weather, Mr. Prim.

MRS. PRIM

I have seen thee wear a handkerchief; nay, and a mask to boot,
in the middle of July.

MRS. LOVELY

Aye, to keep the sun from scorching me.

OBADIAH PRIM

If thou couldst not bear the sunbeams, how dost thou think   50
man should bear thy beams? Those breasts inflame desire; let
them be hid, I say.

MRS. LOVELY

Let me be quiet, I say. Must I be tormented thus forever? Sure
no woman's condition ever equalled mine; foppery, folly, avarice, and hypocrisy are by turns my constant companions,   55
and I must vary shapes as often as a player. I cannot think my
father meant this tyranny! No; you usurp an authority which
he never intended you should take.

---

56 player] actor

OBADIAH PRIM

Hark thee, dost thou call good counsel tyranny? Do I, or my
wife, tyrannize when we desire thee in all love to put off thy   60
tempting attire and veil thy provokers to sin?

MRS. LOVELY

Deliver me, good heaven! Or I shall go distracted. (*Walks
about.*)

MRS. PRIM

So! Now thy pinners are tossed and thy breasts pulled up;
verily they were seen enough before; fie upon the filthy tailor   65
who made them stays.

MRS. LOVELY

I wish I were in my grave! Kill me rather than treat me thus.

OBADIAH PRIM

Kill thee! Ha, ha; thou think'st thou art acting some lewd play
sure; kill thee! Art thou prepared for death, Anne Lovely? No,
no, thou wouldst rather have a husband, Anne. Thou wantest   70
a gilt coach with six lazy fellows behind to flaunt it in the
ring of vanity among the princes and rulers of the land, who
pamper themselves with the fatness thereof; but I will take
care that none shall squander away thy father's estate; thou
shalt marry none such, Anne.   75

MRS. LOVELY

Would you marry me to one of your own canting sect?†

OBADIAH PRIM

Yea, verily, none else shall ever get my consent, I do assure
thee, Anne.

MRS. LOVELY

And I do assure thee, Obadiah, that I will as soon turn papist
and die in a convent.   80

MRS. PRIM

Oh wickedness!

MRS. LOVELY

Oh stupidity!

OBADIAH PRIM

Oh blindness of heart!

---

64 pinners] the lappets of her circular flat cap (pinner), two long streamers that
hang down behind the cap
66 stays] the stiffened under-bodice that shaped the bosom

MRS. LOVELY

> [*Aside to Prim.*] Thou blinder of the world, don't provoke me,
> lest[†] I betray your sanctity and leave your wife to judge of   85
> your purity. What were the emotions of your spirit when you
> squeezed Mary by the hand last night in the pantry, when she
> told you, you bussed so filthily?[†] Ah! You had no aversion to
> naked bosoms when you begged her to show you a little, lit-
> tle, little bit of her delicious bubby. Don't you remember   90
> those words, Mr. Prim?

MRS. PRIM

> What does she say, Obadiah?

OBADIAH PRIM

> She talketh unintelligibly, Sarah. (*Aside.*) Which way did she
> hear this? This should not have reached the ears of the
> wicked ones; verily, it troubleth me.   95

Enter servant.

SERVANT

> Philip Modelove, whom they call Sir Philip, is below, and
> such another with him; shall I send them up?

OBADIAH PRIM

> Yea. (*Exit [servant].*)[†]

Enter Sir Philip and Colonel.

SIR PHILIP

> How dost thou do, Friend Prim. Odso! My she-Friend here
> too! What, you are documenting Miss Nancy, reading her a   100
> lecture upon the pinched coif, I warrent ye.

MRS. PRIM

> I am sure thou never readest her any lecture that was good.
> — My flesh riseth so at these wicked ones that prudence ad-
> viseth me to withdraw from their sight. (*Exit.*)

---

88 bussed] kissed
96 Philip...Sir Philip] the refusal to use honorific titles was another Quaker public
   testimony
99 Friend] the polite Quaker form of address
100 documenting] admonishing in an authoritative or imperious manner

COLONEL

(*Aside.*) Oh! That I could find means to speak to her! How   105
charming she appears! I wish I could get this letter into her
hand.

SIR PHILIP

Well, Miss Cocky, I hope thou hast got the better of them.

MRS. LOVELY

The difficulties of my life are not to be surmounted, Sir
Philip. (*Aside.*) I hate the impertinence of him as much as the   110
stupidity of the other.

OBADIAH PRIM

Verily, Philip, thou wilt spoil this maiden.

SIR PHILIP

I find we still differ in opinion; but that we may none of us
spoil her, prithee, Prim, let us consent to marry her. I have
sent for our brother guardians to meet me here about that   115
very thing. Madam, will you give me leave to recommend a
husband to you? Here's a gentleman which, in my mind, you
can have no objection to. (*Presents the Colonel to her; she looks
another way.*)

MRS. LOVELY

(*Aside.*) Heaven deliver me from the formal and the fantastic   120
fool.

COLONEL

A fine woman, a fine horse, and fine equipage are the finest
things in the universe. And if I am so happy to possess you,
madam, I shall become the envy of mankind, as much as you
outshine your whole sex. (*As he takes her hand to kiss it, he en-*   125
deavors to put the letter into it; she lets it drop; Prim takes it up.)

MRS. LOVELY

(*Turning from him.*) I have no ambition to appear conspicu-
ously ridiculous, sir.

COLONEL

So fall† the hopes of Fainwell.

MRS. LOVELY

(*Aside.*) Ha! Fainwell! 'Tis he! What have I done? Prim has   130
the letter and all will be discovered.

---

108 Miss Cocky] a term of endearment

OBADIAH PRIM

> Friend, I know not thy name, so cannot call thee by it; but thou seest thy letter is unwelcome to the maiden; she will not read it.

MRS. LOVELY

> Nor shall you. (*Snatches the letter.*) I'll tear it in a thousand   135
> pieces and scatter it, as I will the hopes of all those that any of you shall recommend to me. (*Tears the letter.*)

SIR PHILIP

> Ha! Right woman, faith!

COLONEL

> (*Aside.*) Excellent woman.

OBADIAH PRIM

> Friend, thy garb favoreth too much of the vanity of the age   140
> for my approbation; nothing that resembleth Philip Modelove shall I love, mark that; therefore, Friend Philip, bring no more of thy own apes under my roof.

SIR PHILIP

> I am so entirely a stranger to the monsters of thy breed that I shall bring none of them, I am sure.   145

COLONEL

> (*Aside.*) I am likely to have a pretty task by that time I have gone through them all; but she's a city worth taking and egad I'll carry on the siege. If I can but blow up the outworks, I fancy I am pretty secure of the town.

Enter servant.

SERVANT

> (*To Sir Philip.*) Toby Periwinkle and Thomas Tradelove de-   150
> mandeth to see thee.

SIR PHILIP

> Bid them come up.

MRS. LOVELY

> Deliver me from such an inundation of noise and nonsense. [*Aside.*] Oh Fainwell! Whatever thy contrivance is, prosper it heaven; but oh, I fear thou never canst redeem me. (*Exit.*)   155

SIR PHILIP

> *Sic transit gloria mundi.*

---

156 *Sic transit gloria mundi.*] So passes away the glory of the world.

Enter Mr. Periwinkle and Tradelove.

(*Aside to the Colonel.*) These are my brother guardians, Mr.
Fainwell; prithee observe the creatures.

TRADELOVE

Well, Sir Philip, I obey your summons.

PERIWINKLE

Pray, what have you to offer for the good of Mrs. Lovely, Sir   160
Philip?

SIR PHILIP

First, I desire to know what you intend to do with that lady.
Must she be sent to the Indies for a venture, or live to be an
old maid and then entered amongst your curiosities and
shown for a monster, Mr. Periwinkle?   165

COLONEL

(*Aside.*) Humph, curiosities! That must be the virtuoso.

PERIWINKLE

Why, what would you do with her?

SIR PHILIP

I would recommend this gentleman to her for a husband, sir
— a person whom I have picked out from the whole race of
mankind.   170

OBADIAH PRIM

I would advise thee to shuffle him again with the rest of
mankind, for I like him not.

COLONEL

Pray, sir, without offence to your formality, what may be your
objections?

OBADIAH PRIM

Thy person; thy manners; thy dress; thy acquaintance; thy   175
everything, Friend.

SIR PHILIP

You are most particulalry obliging, Friend, ha, ha.

TRADELOVE

What business do you follow, pray, sir?

---

163 sent...venture] sent to India or the West Indies for commercial speculation
164 curiosities] rarities, oddities

COLONEL

(*Aside.*) Humph, by that question he must be the broker. [*To Tradelove.*] Business, sir! The business of a gentleman.   180

TRADELOVE

That is as much to say, you dress fine, feed high, lie with every woman you like, and pay your surgeon's bills better than your tailor's or your butcher's.

COLONEL

The court is much obliged to you, sir, for your character of a gentleman.   185

TRADELOVE

The court, sir! What would the court do without us citizens?

SIR PHILIP

Without your wives and daughters, you mean, Mr. Tradelove?

PERIWINKLE

Have you ever traveled, sir?

COLONEL

[*Aside.*] That question must not be answered now. [*To Periwinkle.*] In books I have, sir.   190

PERIWINKLE

In books? That's fine traveling indeed! Sir Philip, when you present a person I like, he shall have my consent to marry Mrs. Lovely, till then, your servant. (*Exit.*)

COLONEL

(*Aside.*) I'll make you like me before I have done with you, or I am mistaken.   195

TRADELOVE

And when you can convince me that a beau is more useful to my country than a merchant, you shall have mine; till then, you must excuse me. (*Exit.*)

COLONEL

(*Aside.*) So much for trade. I'll fit you too.

SIR PHILIP

In my opinion, this is very inhumane treatment as to the lady,   200
Mr. Prim.

---

182 pay...bills] payment for cures for venereal disease

OBADIAH PRIM

> Thy opinion and mine happens to differ as much as our oc-
> cupations, Friend; business requireth my presence and folly
> thine, and so I must bid thee farewell. (*Exit.*)

SIR PHILIP

> Here's breeding for you, Mr. Fainwell! Gad take me, I'd give   205
> half my estate to see these rascals bit.

COLONEL

> (*Aside.*) I hope to bite you all, if my plots hit.†

ACT III

Scene: the tavern;   [III.i]
Sackbut, and the Colonel
in an Egyptian dress.

SACKBUT

> A lucky beginning, Colonel — you have got the old beau's
> consent.

COLONEL

> Aye, he's a reasonable creature; but the other three will re-
> quire some pains. Shall I pass upon him, think you? Egad, in
> my mind, I look as antique as if I had been preserved in the   5
> ark.

SACKBUT

> Pass upon him! Aye, aye, as roundly as white wine dashed
> with sack does for mountain and sherry, if you have but as-
> surance enough.

COLONEL

> I have no apprehension from that quarter; assurance is the   10
> cockade of a soldier.

---

206 bit] gotten the better of, cheated
SD: *an Egyptian dress*] probably the conventional theatrical costume for
    Middle-Eastern characters: a long robe, baggy breeches, and a turban
8 mountain] a variety of Malaga white wine made from grapes grown in the
    mountains

SACKBUT

> Aye, but the assurance of a soldier differs much from that of a traveler. Can you lie with a good grace?

COLONEL

> As heartily, when my mistress is the prize, as I would meet the foe when my country called and king commanded; so don't 15
> you fear that part; if he don't know me again, I'm safe. I hope he'll come.

SACKBUT

> I wish all my debts would come as sure. I told him you had been a great traveler, had many valuable curiosities, and was a person of a most singular taste; he seemed transported and 20
> begged me to keep you till he came.

COLONEL

> Aye, aye, he need not fear my running away. Let's have a bottle of sack, landlord, our ancestors drank sack.

SACKBUT

> You shall have it.

COLONEL

> And whereabouts is the trap door you mentioned? 25

SACKBUT

> There's the conveyance, sir. (*Exit.*)

COLONEL

> Now if I should cheat all these roguish guardians and carry off my mistress in triumph, it would be what the French call a *grand coup d'éclat*. Odso! Here comes Periwinkle. Ah! Deuce take this beard; pray Jupiter it does not give me the slip and 30
> spoil all.

Enter Sackbut with wine, and Periwinkle following.

SACKBUT

> Sir, this gentleman, hearing you have been a great traveler and a person of fine speculation, begs leave to take a glass with you; he is a man of a curious taste himself.

---

29 *grand...d'éclat*] great feat
33 speculation] profound, conjectural reasoning

COLONEL

> The gentleman has it in his face and garb: sir, you are wel- 35
> come.

PERIWINKLE

> Sir, I honor a traveler and men of your inquiring disposition.
> The oddness of your habit pleases me extremely; 'tis very an-
> tique, and for that I like it.

COLONEL

> It is very antique, sir. This habit once belonged to the famous 40
> Claudius Ptolemeus, who lived in the year a hundred and
> thirty-five.

SACKBUT

> (*Aside.*) If he keeps up to the sample, he shall lie with the
> devil for a bean-stack and win it every straw.

PERIWINKLE

> A hundred and thirty-five! Why, that's prodigious now. Well, 45
> certainly 'tis the finest thing in the world to be a traveler.

COLONEL

> For my part, I value none of the modern fashions of a fig-leaf.

PERIWINKLE

> No more do I, sir; I had rather be the jest of a fool, than his
> favorite. I am laughed at here for my singularity. This coat,
> you must know, sir, was formerly worn by that ingenious and 50
> very learned person, John Tradescant.

COLONEL

> John Tradescant! Let me embrace you, Sir. John Tradescant
> was my uncle, by mother-side; and I thank you for the honor
> you do his memory; he was a very curious man indeed.

PERIWINKLE

> Your uncle, sir! Nay then, 'tis no wonder that your taste is so 55
> refined; why, you have it in your blood. My humble service
> to you, sir, to the immortal memory of John Tradescant, your
> never-to-be-forgotten uncle. (*Drinks.*)

---

41 Claudius Ptolemeus] famous Greek astronomer, mathematician, and
geographer of Alexandria, also known as Ptolemy
51 John Tradsescant] (1608-1662) traveler, naturalist, and gardener; his collection
of natural curiosities was famous and became the basis of the Ashmolean
Museum

COLONEL

Give me a glass, landlord.

PERIWINKLE

I find you are primitive even in your wine; canary was the   60
drink of our wise forefathers; 'tis balsamic and saves the
charge of apothecaries' cordials. Oh! that I had lived in your
uncle's days! Or rather, that he was now alive. Oh! How
proud he'd be of such a nephew!

SACKBUT

(*Aside.*) Oh pox! That would have spoiled the jest.   65

PERIWINKLE

A person of your curiosity must have collected many rarities.

COLONEL

I have some, sir, which are not yet come ashore, as an Egyptian's idol.

PERIWINKLE

Pray, what might that be?

COLONEL

It is, sir, a kind of an ape, which they formerly worshipped in   70
that country; I took it from the breast of a female mummy.

PERIWINKLE

Ha, ha! Our women retain part of their idolatry to this day,
for many an ape lies on a lady's breast, ha, ha —

SACKBUT

(*Aside.*) A smart old thief.

COLONEL

Two tusks of a hippopotamus,[†] two pair of Chinese nut-   75
crackers, and one Egyptian mummy.

PERIWINKLE

Pray, sir, have you never a crocodile?

COLONEL

Humph! The boatswain brought one with design to show it,
but touching at Rotterdam and hearing it was no rarity in
England, he sold it to a Dutch poet.   80

SACKBUT

The devil's in that nation, it rivals us in everything.

---

60 canary] a light, sweet wine from the Canary Islands
61 balsamic] soothing, restorative

PERIWINKLE

I should have been very glad to have seen a living crocodile.

COLONEL

My genius led me to things more worthy of my regard. Sir, I have seen the utmost limits of this globular world; I have seen the sun rise and set; know in what degree of heat he is at 85 noon to the breadth of a hair and what quantity of combustibles he burns in a day, how much of it turns to ashes and how much to cinders.

PERIWINKLE

To cinders? You amaze me, sir; I never heard that the sun consumed anything. Descartes[†] tells us — 90

COLONEL

Descartes,[†] with the rest of his brethren both ancient and modern, knew nothing of the matter. I tell you, sir, that nature admits an annual decay, though imperceptible to vulgar eyes. Sometimes his rays destroy below, sometimes above. You have heard of blazing comets, I suppose? 95

PERIWINKLE

Yes, yes, I remember to have seen one; and our astrologers tell us of another which shall happen very quickly.

COLONEL

Those comets are little islands bordering on the sun, which at certain times are set on fire by that luminous body's moving over them perpendicular, which will one day occasion a gen- 100 eral conflagration.

SACKBUT

(*Aside.*) One need not scruple the Colonel's capacity, faith.

PERIWINKLE

This is marvellous strange! These cinders are what I never read of in any of our learned dissertations.

COLONEL

(*Aside.*) I don't know how the devil you should. 105

---

90 Descartes] René Descartes (1596-1650) wrote about sun spots in his unfinished scientific work, *The World*

96-7 astrologers...quickly] "astrologers" for "astronomers"; in 1705 Edmund Halley predicted the return of the comet he had observed in 1682

SACKBUT

(*Aside.*) He has it at his fingers' ends; one would swear he had 105
learned to lie at school, he does it so cleverly.

PERIWINKLE

Well, you travelers see strange things! Pray, sir, have you any
of those cinders?

COLONEL

I have, among my other curiosities. 110

PERIWINKLE

Oh, what have I lost for want of traveling! Pray, what have
you else?

COLONEL

Several things worth your attention. I have a muff made of
the feathers of those geese that saved the Roman Capitol.

PERIWINKLE

Is't possible? 115

SACKBUT

(*Aside.*) Yes, if you are such a goose to believe him.

COLONEL

I have an Indian leaf, which open will cover an acre of land,
yet folds up into so little a compass, you may put it into your
snuffbox.

SACKBUT

(*Aside.*) Humph! That's a thunderer. 120

PERIWINKLE

Amazing!

COLONEL

Ah! Mine is but a little one; I have seen some of them that
would cover one of the Caribbean[†] islands.

PERIWINKLE

Well, if I don't travel before I die, I shan't rest in my grave.
Pray, what do the Indians with them? 125

COLONEL

Sir, they use them in their wars for tents, the old women for
riding hoods, the young for fans and umbrellas.

SACKBUT

(*Aside.*) He has a fruitful invention.

---

114 geese...Capitol] according to Roman legend, the cackling of the geese in
Juno's temple saved the Capitol from invaders by warning the guards

PERIWINKLE

    I admire our East India Company imports none of them,
they would certainly find their account in them.   130

COLONEL

    (*Aside*.) Right, if they could find the leaves. [*To Periwinkle.*]
Look ye, sir, do you see this little vial?

PERIWINKLE

    Pray you, what is it?

COLONEL

    This is called *poluflosboio*.

PERIWINKLE

    Poluflosboio! It has a rumbling sound.   135

COLONEL

    Right, sir, it proceeds from a rumbling nature. This water was
part of those waves which bore Cleopatra's vessel when she
sailed to meet Anthony.

PERIWINKLE

    Well, of all that ever traveled, none had a taste like you.

COLONEL

    But here's the wonder of the world. This, sir, is called, *zona* or   140
moros musphonon, the virtues of this is inestimable.

PERIWINKLE

    Moros musphonon! What in the name of wisdom can that be?
To me it seems a plain belt.

COLONEL

    This girdle has carried me all the world over.

PERIWINKLE

    You have carried it, you mean.   145

COLONEL

    I mean as I say, sir. Whenever I am girded with this, I am in-
visible; and by turning this little screw can be in the court of

---

129 East India Company] joint-stock trading company with the monopoly on
    trade with the Indies, East (i.e. India) and West, and with Asia

134 *poluflosboio*] (Greek) loud-roaring, boisterous

140 *zona*] Latin form of the Greek word *zone*, meaning girdle

141 *moros musphonon*] fanciful Greek; Stathas conjecturally translates it as
    "mousetrap for a fool" (n. to Act III, l. 148)

the Great Mogul, the Grand Seignior, and King George in as
little time as your cook can poach an egg.

PERIWINKLE

You must pardon me, sir, I can't believe it. 150

COLONEL

If my landlord pleases, he shall try the experiment immediately.

SACKBUT

I thank you kindly, sir, but I have no inclination to ride post
to the devil.

COLONEL

No, no, you shan't stir a foot, I'll only make you invisible.

SACKBUT

But if you could not make me visible again? 155

PERIWINKLE

Come try it upon me, sir, I am not afraid of the devil nor all
his tricks. Zbud, I'll stand 'em all.

COLONEL

There, sir, put it on. Come, landlord, you and I must face the
east.
They turn about.

Is it on, sir?

PERIWINKLE 160

'Tis on.
They turn about again.

SACKBUT

Heaven protect me! Where is he?

PERIWINKLE

Why here, just where I was.

SACKBUT

Where, where, in the name of virtue? Ah, poor Mr. Periwinkle! Egad, look to't, you had best, sir, and let him be seen
again, or I shall have you burnt for a wizard.

COLONEL 165

Have patience, good landlord.

---

148 Great Mogul] the Emperor of Delhi
148 Grand Seignior] the Sultan of Turkey

PERIWINKLE

But really, don't you see me now?

SACKBUT

No more than I see my grandmother that died forty years
ago.   170

PERIWINKLE

Are you sure you don't lie? Methinks I stand just where I did
and see you as plain as I did before.

SACKBUT

Ah! I wish I could see you once again.

COLONEL

Take off the girdle, sir.

He takes it off.

SACKBUT

Ah, sir, I am glad to see you with all my heart. (*Embraces*   175
him.)

PERIWINKLE

This is very odd, certainly there must be some trick in't. Pray,
sir, will you do me the favor to put it on yourself?

COLONEL

With all my heart.

PERIWINKLE

But first I'll secure the door.

COLONEL   180

You know how to turn the screw, Mr. Sackbut.

SACKBUT

Yes, yes. Come Mr. Periwinkle. we must turn full east.
They turn; the Colonel sinks down a trapdoor.

COLONEL

'Tis done; now turn.

They turn.

PERIWINKLE

Ha! Mercy upon me! My flesh creeps upon my bones. This
must be a conjurer, Mr. Sackbut.

SACKBUT

He is the devil, I think.   185

PERIWINKLE

Oh! Mr. Sackbut, why do you name the devil when perhaps he may be at your elbow.

SACKBUT

At my elbow! Marry, heaven forbid.

COLONEL

(*Below.*) Are you satisfied, sir?

PERIWINKLE

Yes, sir, yes. How hollow his voice sounds!   190

SACKBUT

Yours seemed just the same. Faith, I wish this girdle were mine, I'd sell wine no more. Hark ye, Mr. Periwinkle (*takes him aside until the Colonel rises again*), if he would sell this girdle, you might travel with great expedition.

COLONEL

But it is not to be parted with for money.   195

PERIWINKLE

I am sorry for't, sir, because I think it the greatest curiosity I ever heard of.

COLONEL

By the advice of a learned physiognomist in Grand Cairo, who consulted the lines in my face, I returned to England, where he told me I should find a rarity in the keeping of four   200 men, which I was born to possess for the benefit of mankind, and the first of the four that gave me his consent, I should present him with this girdle. Till I have found this jewel, I shall not part with the girdle.

PERIWINKLE

What can that rarity be? Did he not name it to you?   205

COLONEL

Yes, sir; he called it a chaste, beautiful, unaffected woman.

PERIWINKLE

Pish! Women are no rarities. I never had any great taste that way. I married, indeed, to please a father and I got a girl to please my wife; but she and the child (thank heaven) died together. Women are the very gewgaws of the creation; play-   210

---

210 gewgaws] toys

things for boys, which, when they write man, they ought to throw aside.

SACKBUT

(*Aside.*) A fine lecture to be read to a circle of ladies!

PERIWINKLE

What woman is there, dressed in all the pride and foppery of the times, can boast of such a foretop as the cockatoo?† 215

COLONEL

(*Aside.*) I must humor him. [*Aloud.*] Such a skin as the lizard?

PERIWINKLE

Such a shining breast as the hummingbird?

COLONEL

Such a shape as the antelope?

PERIWINKLE

Or, in all the artful mixture of their various dresses, have they half the beauty of one box of butterflies? 220

COLONEL

No, that must be allowed. For my part, if it were not for the benefit of mankind, I'd have nothing to do with them, for they are as indifferent to me as a sparrow or a flesh-fly.

PERIWINKLE

Pray, sir, what benefit is the world to reap from this lady?

COLONEL

Why, sir, she is to bear me a son, who shall restore the art of 225 embalming and the old Roman manner of burying their dead; and, for the benefit of posterity, he is to discover the longitude, so long sought for in vain.

PERIWINKLE

Od! These are very valuable things, Mr. Sackbut.

SACKBUT

(*Aside.*) He hits it off admirably and t'other swallows it like 230 sack and sugar. [*Aloud.*] Certainly this lady must be your ward, Mr. Periwinkle, by her being under the care of four persons.

---

215 foretop] hair arranged on the forehead; by analogy, the cockatoo's crest

227-8 discover the longitude] in 1714 Parliament had passed a bill offering a prize of £20,000 for the first person to develop an accurate way of finding the longitude at sea

PERIWINKLE

By the description it should. (*Aside.*) Egad, if I could get that girdle, I'd ride with the sun and make the tour of the whole world in four-and-twenty hours. [*To the Colonel.*] And are you to give that girdle to the first of the four guardians that shall give his consent to marry that lady, say you, sir? 235

COLONEL

I am so ordered, when I can find him.

PERIWINKLE

I fancy I know the very woman — her name is Anne Lovely. 240

COLONEL

Excellent! He said, indeed, that the first letter of her name was *L*.

PERIWINKLE

Did he really? Well, that's prodigiously amazing, that a person in Grand Cairo should know anything of my ward.

COLONEL

Your ward? 245

PERIWINKLE

To be plain with you, sir, I am one of those four guardians.

COLONEL

Are you indeed, sir? I am transported to find the man who is to possess† this *moros musphonon* is a person of so curious a taste. Here is a writing drawn up by that famous Egyptian, which, if you will please to sign, you must turn your face full north, and the girdle is yours. 250

PERIWINKLE

If I live till this boy is born, I'll be embalmed and sent to the Royal Society when I die.

COLONEL

That you shall most certainly.

Enter drawer.

DRAWER

Here's Mr. Staytape the tailor, inquires for you, Colonel. 255

---

253 Royal Society] scientific society founded by Royal Charter in 1662

SACKBUT

Who do you speak to, you son of a whore?

PERIWINKLE

(*Aside.*) Ha! Colonel!

COLONEL

(*Aside.*) Confound the blundering dog!

DRAWER

Why, to Colonel —

SACKBUT

Get you out, you rascal. (*Kicks him out and exit after him.*)   260

DRAWER

[*As he exits.*] What the devil is the matter?

COLONEL

(*Aside.*) This dog has ruined all my scheme, I see by Periwinkle's looks.

PERIWINKLE

How finely I should have been choused. Colonel, you'll pardon me that I did not give you your title before — it was   265
pure ignorance, faith it was. Pray — hem, hem — pray, Colonel, what post had this learned Egyptian in your regiment?

COLONEL

(*Aside.*) A pox of your sneer. [*To Periwinkle.*] I don't understand you, sir.

PERIWINKLE

No? That's strange! I understand you, Colonel. An Egyptian   270
of Grand Cairo! Ha, ha, ha. I am sorry such a well-invented
tale should do you no more service. We old fellows can see as
far into a millstone as him that picks it. I am not to be tricked
out of my trust, mark that.

COLONEL

(*Aside.*) The devil! I must carry it off; I wish I were fairly out.   275
[*To Periwinkle.*] Look ye, sir, you may make what jest you
please — but the stars will be obeyed, sir, and, depend upon
it, I shall have the lady and you none of the girdle. (*Aside.*)
Now for Freeman's part of the plot. (*Exit.*)

---

264 choused] swindled
272-3 We...it.] proverbial, often ironic, claim to acuteness

PERIWINKLE

> The stars! Ha, ha. No star has favored you, it seems. The gir- 280
> dle! Ha, ha, ha, none of your legerdemain tricks can pass
> upon me. Why, what a pack of trumpery has this rogue
> picked up? His *pagod,*† *poluflosboios,* his *zonas, moros
> musphonons,* and the devil knows what. But I'll take care —
> Ha! Gone? — Aye, 'twas time to sneak off — Soho! The 285
> house! (*Enter Sackbut.*) Where is this trickster? Send for a
> constable, I'll have this rascal before the Lord Mayor; I'll
> Grand Cairo him, with a pox to him. I believe you had a
> hand in putting this imposture upon me, Sackbut.

SACKBUT

> Who, I, Mr. Periwinkle? I scorn it; I perceived he was a cheat 290
> and left the room on purpose to send a constable to appre-
> hend him, and endeavored to stop him when he went out —
> but the rogue made but one step from the stairs to the door,
> called a coach, leapt into it, and drove away like the devil, as
> Mr. Freeman can witness, who is at the bar and desires to 295
> speak with you; he is this minute come to town.

PERIWINKLE

> Send him in. (*Exit Sackbut.*) What a scheme this rogue had
> laid! How I should have been laughed at, had it succeeded!
> (*Enter Freeman booted and spurred.*) Mr. Freeman, your dress
> commands your welcome to town; what will you drink? I 300
> had like to have been imposed upon here by the veriest rascal
> —

FREEMAN

> I am sorry to hear it. The dog flew for't — he had not 'scaped
> me if I had been aware of him; Sackbut struck at him, but
> missed his blow, or he had done his business for him. 305

PERIWINKLE

> I believe you never heard of such a contrivance, Mr. Freeman,
> as this fellow had found out.

FREEMAN

> Mr. Sackbut has told me the whole story, Mr. Periwinkle; but
> now I have something to tell you of much more importance
> to yourself. I happened to lie one night at Coventry, and 310

283 *pagod*] idol

knowing your uncle, Sir Toby Periwinkle, I paid him a visit, and to my great surprise found him dying.

PERIWINKLE

Dying!

FREEMAN

Dying, in all appearance; the servants weeping, the room in darkness; the apothecary, shaking his head, told me the doctors had given him over, and then there is small hopes, you know.   315

PERIWINKLE

I hope he has made his will. He always told me he would make me his heir.

FREEMAN

I have heard you say as much and therefore resolved to give you notice. I should think it would not be amiss if you went down tomorrow morning.   320

PERIWINKLE

It is a long journey, and the roads very bad.

FREEMAN

But he has a great estate, and the land very good. Think upon that.   325

PERIWINKLE

Why, that's true, as you say; I'll think upon it. In the meantime, I give you many thanks for your civility, Mr. Freeman, and should be glad of your company to dine with me.

FREEMAN

I am obliged to be at Jonathan's Coffee-house at two, and it is now half-an-hour after one; if I dispatch my business, I'll wait on you; I know your hour.   330

PERIWINKLE

You shall be very welcome, Mr. Freeman; and so, your humble servant. (*Exit.*)

Re-enter Colonel and Sackbut.

---

329 Jonathan's Coffee-house] in Exchange Alley near the Royal Exchange; center for speculators; the forerunner of the Stock Exchange

FREEMAN

    Ha, ha, ha — I have done your business, Colonel; he has swallowed the bait.   335

COLONEL

    I overheard all, though I am a little in the dark. I am to personate a highwayman, I suppose. That's a project I am not fond of; for though I may fright him out of his consent, he may fright me out of my life when he discovers me, as he certainly must in the end.   340

FREEMAN

    No, no, I have a plot for you without danger; but first we must manage Tradelove. Has the tailor brought your clothes?

SACKBUT

    Yes, pox take the thief.

COLONEL

    Pox take your drawer for a jolt-headed rogue.

FREEMAN

    Well, well, no matter, I warrant we have him yet. But now   345
you must put on the Dutch merchant.

COLONEL

    The deuce of this trading-plot. I wish he had been an old soldier, that I might have attacked him in my own way, heard him fight over all the battles of the Civil War — but for trade, by Jupiter, I shall never do it.   350

SACKBUT

    Never fear, Colonel, Mr. Freeman will instruct you.

FREEMAN

    You'll see what others do, the coffee-house will instruct you.

COLONEL

    I must venture, however. But I have a farther plot in my head upon Tradelove, which you must assist me in, Freeman; you are in credit with him, I heard you say.   355

FREEMAN

    I am, and will scruple nothing to serve you, Colonel.

COLONEL

    Come along then. Now for the Dutchman. Honest Ptolemy, by your leave,

---

339 fright...life] because highway robbery was punishable by death

Now must bob wig and business come in play,
And a fair thirty-thousand-pounder leads the way.†

ACT IV

*Scene: Jonathan's Coffee-house in Exchange Alley. Crowd of people with
rolls of paper and parchment in their hands; a bar, and coffee-boys waiting.*

*Enter Tradelove and stockjobbers
with rolls of paper and parchment.*

FIRST STOCKJOBBER
South Sea at seven-eighths! Who buys?

SECOND STOCKJOBBER
South Sea bonds due at Michaelmas, 1718. Class lottery tickets.

THIRD STOCKJOBBER
East India bonds?

FOURTH STOCKJOBBER
What, all sellers and no buyers? Gentlemen, I'll buy a thou-   5
sand pound for Tuesday next at three-fourths.†

COFFEE-BOY
Fresh coffee, gentlemen, fresh coffee?

TRADELOVE
Hark ye, Gabriel, you'll pay the difference of that stock we
transacted for t'other day.

---

359 bob wig] a simple, undress wig

SD *rolls...parchment*] for recording stock transactions

SD *stockjobbers*] traders in stock; interchangeable with "brokers" in popular
terminology

1 South Sea at seven-eighths] stock in the South Sea Company, a chartered
joint-stock trading company, like the East India Company, with the
monopoly on English trade with South America and the Pacific; founded in
1711, mainly to fund the national debt. Stock prices were conventionally
quoted in eighths; only the final fraction is quoted

2 Michaelmas] Feast of St. Michael, 29 September; one of the four quarter days of
the business year, on which financial transactions were completed

2-3 Class lottery tickets] one of the lotteries run by the government to fund the
national debt; tickets were divided into classes with different prizes for each

GABRIEL

Aye, Mr. Tradelove, here's a note for the money upon the   10
Sword Blade Company. (*Gives him a note.*)

COFFEE-BOY

Bohea tea, gentlemen?

Enter a Man.

MAN

Is Mr. Smuggle here?

FIRST COFFEE-BOY

Mr. Smuggle's not here, sir, you'll find him at the books.

SECOND STOCKJOBBER

Ho! Here come[†] two sparks from the other end of the town,   15
what news bring they?

Enter two Gentlemen.

TRADELOVE

I would fain bite that spark in the brown coat, he comes very
often into the Alley, but never employs a broker.

Enter Colonel and Freeman.

SECOND STOCKJOBBER

Who does anything in the Civil List lottery? Or caco?
Zounds, where are all the Jews this afternoon? Are you a bull   20
or a bear today, Abraham?

---

11 Sword Blade Company] the major stock brokerage firm of the time and banker
for the South Sea Company

14 at the books] "presumably the [stock] transfer books at the Bank, South Sea
House, etc." (Dickson 503)

15 sparks] elegant young men

19 Civil...lottery] a government lottery (1713) to discharge the debts of the royal
household

19 caco] probably cocoa beans

20 Jews] many jobbers and brokers were Jews, but prejudice reinforced the
association between Jews and the market

21 a bull or a bear] bull, a speculative purchaser for a rise in stock prices; bear, a
speculator for a fall in prices, who sells stock he does not yet own in the hope
that he will be able to buy it at a lower price before the delivery date

THIRD STOCKJOBBER

A bull, faith — but I have a good put for next week.

TRADELOVE

Mr. Freeman, your servant! Who is that gentleman?

FREEMAN

A Dutch merchant, just come to England; but hark ye, Mr. Tradelove, I have a piece of news will get you as much as the   25 French king's death did, if you are expeditious.

TRADELOVE

Say you so, sir! Pray, what is it?

FREEMAN

(*Showing him a letter.*) Read there, I received it just now from one that belongs to the Emperor's minister.

TRADELOVE

(*Reads.*) Sir, As I have many obligations to you, I cannot miss   30 any opportunity to show my gratitude; this moment my Lord has received a private express that the Spaniards have raised their siege from before Cagliari; if this prove any advantage to you, it will answer both the ends and wishes of, sir, your most obliged humble servant, Henricus Dusseldorp. Post-   35 script, In two or three hours the news will be public. (*Aside to Freeman.*) May one depend upon this, Mr. Freeman?

FREEMAN

You may. I never knew this person send me a false piece of news in my life.

TRADELOVE

Sir, I am much obliged to you. Egad, 'tis rare news. — Who   40 sells South Sea for next week?

STOCKJOBBERS

(*All together.*†) I sell; I, I, I, I, I sell.

---

22 put] the option of delivering a particular amount of stock at a certain price within a specified time

29 Emperor's] Charles VI, Emperor of Austria

33 siege...Cagliari] Cagliari is the capital of Sardinia, taken from Spain and given to Austria by the Peace of Utrecht; Spain had invaded Sardinia in August 1717, provoking a crisis in the Mediterranean

41 South Sea] the South Sea Company traded with the Spanish empire; the price of its stock is shown here "as highly dependant on...news from Spain, the country with the power to control the company's trade and therefore its profits..." (Dickson 503)

FIRST STOCKJOBBER

I'll sell five thousand pounds[†] for next week at five-eighths.

SECOND STOCKJOBBER

I'll sell ten thousand at five-eighths for the same time.

TRADELOVE

Nay, nay, hold, hold, not all together,[†] gentlemen, I'll be no 45
bull, I'll buy no more than I can take. Will you sell ten thousand pound at a half for any day next week, except Saturday?

FIRST STOCKJOBBER

I'll sell it you, Mr. Tradelove.

FREEMAN

(*Whispers to one of the gentlemen.*)

GENTLEMAN

(*Aloud.*) The Spaniards raised the siege of Cagliari! I don't be- 50
lieve one word of it.

SECOND GENTLEMAN

Raised the siege! As much as you have raised the Monument.

FREEMAN

'Tis raised, I assure you, sir.

SECOND GENTLEMAN

What will you lay on't?

FREEMAN

What you please. 55

FIRST GENTLEMAN

Why, I have a brother upon the spot in the Emperor's service;
I am certain if there were any such thing, I should have had a
letter.

A STOCKJOBBER

How's this? The siege of Cagliari raised; I wish it may be true,
'twill make business stir and stocks rise. 60

FIRST STOCKJOBBER

Tradelove's a cunning fat bear; if this news proves true, I shall
repent I sold him the five thousand pounds. — Pray, sir, what
assurance have you that the siege is raised?

---

52 Monument] a column designed by Christopher Wren commemorating the
Great Fire of 1666

62 five thousand pounds] ten thousand according to the first stockjobber's revised
offer to Tradelove

FREEMAN

There is come an express to the Emperor's minister.

SECOND STOCKJOBBER

I'll know that presently. (*Exit.*)   65

FIRST GENTLEMAN

Let it come where it will, I'll hold you fifty pounds 'tis false.

FREEMAN

'Tis done.

SECOND GENTLEMAN

I'll lay you a brace of hundreds upon the same.

FREEMAN

I'll take you.

FOURTH STOCKJOBBER

Egad, I'll hold twenty pieces 'tis not raised, sir.   70

FREEMAN

Done with you too.

TRADELOVE

I'll lay any man a brace of thousands the siege is raised.

FREEMAN

(*Aside to Tradelove.*) The Dutch merchant is your man to take
in.

TRADELOVE

Does not he know the news?   75

FREEMAN

(*To Tradelove.*) Not a syllable; if he did, he would bet a hundred thousand pound as soon as one penny; he's plaguy rich,
and a mighty man at wagers.

TRADELOVE

Say you so. — Egad, I'll bite him if possible. — Are you from
Holland, sir?   80

COLONEL

Ya, mynheer.

TRADELOVE

Had you the news before you came away?

COLONEL

Wat believe you, mynheer?

---

81 Ya, mynheer] Yes, sir.
83 Wat...mynheer?] What do you believe, sir?

TRADELOVE

What do I believe? Why, I believe that the Spaniards have actually raised the siege of Cagliari.   85

COLONEL

Wat duyvels niews is dat? 'Tis niet waer, mynheer — 'tis no true, sir.

TRADELOVE

'Tis so true, mynheer, that I'll lay you two thousand pounds upon it. [*Aside to Freeman.*] You are sure the letter may be depended upon, Mr. Freeman?   90

FREEMAN

(*Aside to Tradelove.*) Do you think I would venture my money if I were not sure of the truth of it?

COLONEL

Two duysend pond, mynheer, 'tis gedaen — dis gentleman sal hold de gelt.[†] (*Gives Freeman money.*)

TRADELOVE

With all my heart — this binds the wager.[†] You have certainly lost, mynheer, the siege is raised indeed.   95

COLONEL

Ik gelove't niet, Mynheer Freeman, ik sal ye dubbled houden, if you please.

FREEMAN

I am let into the secret, therefore won't win your money.

TRADELOVE

Ha, ha, ha! I have snapped the Dutchman, faith, ha, ha! This is   100
no ill day's work. — Pray, may I crave your name, mynheer?

COLONEL

Myn naem, mynheer! Myn naem is Jan van Timtamtirelire-letta[†] Heer van Fainwell.

TRADELOVE

Zounds, 'tis a damned long name, I shall never remember it — Mynheer van Tim, Tim, Tim — What the devil is it?   105

---

86 wat duyvels...mynheer] What devil's news is that? 'Tis not true, sir.

93-4 Two duysend...gelt.] Two thousand pound, sir, 'tis done — this gentleman shall hold the money.

97 Ik...houden] I don't like it, Mister Freeman, I shall hold you doubled

FREEMAN

> Oh! Never heed, I know the gentleman and will pass my
> word for twice the sum.

TRADELOVE

> That's enough.

COLONEL

> [*Aside.*] You'll hear of me sooner than you'll wish old gentle-
> man, I fancy. (*Aside [to Freeman].*) You'll come to Sackbut's,   110
> Freeman? (*Exit.*)

FREEMAN

> (*Aside to the Colonel.*) Immediately.

FIRST MAN

> Humphrey† Hump here?

SECOND COFFEE-BOY

> Mr. Humphrey† Hump is not here; you'll find him upon the
> Dutch walk.   115

TRADELOVE

> Mr. Freeman, I give you many thanks for your kindness.

FREEMAN

> (*Aside.*) I fear you'll repent when you know all.

TRADELOVE

> Will you dine with me?

FREEMAN

> I am engaged at Sackbut's; adieu. (*Exit.*)

TRADELOVE

> Sir, your humble servant. Now I'll see what I can do upon   120
> Change with my news. (*Exit.*)

---

115 Dutch walk] meeting place for Dutch merchants in the courtyard of the
  Royal Exchange
121 Change] the Royal Exchange

Scene: the tavern.

Enter Freeman and Colonel.

FREEMAN

Ha, ha, ha! The old fellow swallowed the bait as greedily as a gudgeon.

COLONEL

I have him, faith, ha, ha, ha. His two thousand pound's secure — if he would keep his money, he must part with the lady, ha, ha. What came of your two friends? They performed their 5 part very well; you should have brought 'em to take a glass with us.

FREEMAN

No matter, we'll drink a bottle together another time. I did not care to bring them hither; there's no necessity to trust them with the main secret, you know, Colonel. 10

COLONEL

Nay, that's right, Freeman.

Enter Sackbut.

SACKBUT

Joy, joy, Colonel, the luckiest accident in the world!

COLONEL

What say'st thou?

SACKBUT

This letter does your business.

COLONEL

(*Reads.*) To Obadiah Prim, hosier, near the building called the 15 Monument, in London.

FREEMAN

A letter to Prim; how came you by it?

SACKBUT

Looking over the letters our post-woman brought, as I always do, to see what letters are directed to my house (for she can't read you must know), I spied this to Prim, so paid for't 20

---

2 gudgeon] a small fish; fig. one that will bite at any bait, a gullible person

among the rest; I have given the old jade a pint of wine on
purpose to delay time, till you see if the letter will be of any
service; then I'll seal it up again and tell her I took it by mistake; I have read it and fancy you'll like the project — read,
read, Colonel.   25

COLONEL

(*Reads.*) Friend Prim, There is arrived from Pennsylvania[†]
one Simon Pure, a leader of the faithful, who hath sojourned
with us eleven days and hath been of great comfort to the
brethren. He intendeth for the quarterly meeting in London;
I have recommended him to thy house; I pray thee intreat   30
him kindly and let thy wife cherish him, for he's of weakly
constitution. He will depart from us the third day; which is
all from thy Friend in the faith, Aminadab Holdfast. Ha, ha!
Excellent! I understand you, landlord, I am to personate this
Simon Pure, am I not?   35

SACKBUT

Don't you like the hint?

COLONEL

Admirably well!

FREEMAN

'Tis the best contrivance in the world, if the right Simon gets
not there before you.

COLONEL

No, no, the Quakers never ride post; he can't be here before   40
tomorrow at soonest. Do you send and buy me a Quaker's
dress, Mr. Sackbut[†]; and suppose, Freeman, you should wait at
the Bristol coach, that if you see any such person, you might
contrive to give me notice.

FREEMAN

I will — the country dress and boots, are they ready?   45

---

29 quarterly meeting] meeting for delegates from local monthly meetings
   throughout a county, held four times a year
30 intreat] treat
32 third day] Tuesday; Quakers designated the days of the week in this way to
   accord with Biblical practice in Genesis and to avoid the conventional
   designations derived from the names of the pagan gods
33 Aminadab] a generic satirical name for a Quaker
41-2 a Quaker's dress] for a man this meant a very plain, dark-colored coat with
   narrow cuffs, a narrow cravat, a broad-brimmed hat, and a loose cloak

SACKBUT

Yes, yes, everything, sir.

FREEMAN

Bring 'em in then. (*Exit Sackbut.*) Thou must dispatch Peri-winkle first. Remember his uncle, Sir Toby Periwinkle,† is an old bachelor of seventy-five; that he has seven hundred a year, most in abbey land; that he was once in love with your   50
mother, and shrewdly suspected by some to be your father; that you have been thirty years his steward, and ten years his gentleman — remember to improve these hints.

COLONEL

Never fear, let me alone for that — but what's the steward's name?   55

FREEMAN

His name is Pillage.

COLONEL

Enough. (*Enter Sackbut with clothes.*) Now for the country put. (*Dresses.*)

FREEMAN

Egad, landlord, thou deservest to have the first night's lodging with the lady for thy fidelity. What say you, Colonel, shall we   60
settle a club here, you'll make one?

COLONEL

Make one? I'll bring a set of honest officers, that will spend their money as freely to their King's health as they would their blood in his service.

SACKBUT

I thank you, Colonel. (*Bell rings.*) Here, here. (*Exit Sackbut.*)   65

COLONEL

So now for my boots. (*Puts on boots.*) Shall I find you here, Freeman, when I come back?

FREEMAN

Yes, or I'll leave word with Sackbut where you may send for me. Have you the writings? The will, and everything?

COLONEL

All, all!   70

---

50 abbey land] part of the estate of an abbey before the dissolution of the monasteries at the Reformation
57-8 country put] bumpkin

Enter Sackbut.

SACKBUT

Zounds! Mr. Freeman! Yonder is Tradelove in the damned'st passion in the world. He swears you are in the house — he says you told him you was to dine here.

FREEMAN

I did so. Ha, ha, ha! He has found himself bit already.

COLONEL

The devil! He must not see me in this dress. 75

SACKBUT

I told him I expected you here, but you were not come yet.

FREEMAN

Very well — make you haste out, Colonel, and let me alone to deal with him. Where is he?

SACKBUT

In the King's Head.

COLONEL

You remember what I told you? 80

FREEMAN

Aye, aye, very well, landlord; let him know I am come in. And now, Mr. Pillage, success attend you.

Exit Sackbut.

COLONEL

Mr. Proteus, rather.
From changing shape and imitating Jove,
I draw the happy omens of my love. 85
I'm not the first young brother of the blade
Who made his fortune in a masquerade. (*Exit Colonel.*)

Enter Tradelove.

FREEMAN

Zounds! Mr. Tradelove, we're bit it seems.

---

83 Proteus] shape-changing god
84 changing...Jove] Jupiter adopted a variety of disguises to seduce mortal women

TRADELOVE

Bit do you call it, Mr. Freeman, I am ruined. Pox on your news. 90

FREEMAN

Pox on the rascal that sent it me.

TRADELOVE

Sent it you! Why Gabriel Skinflint has been at the minister's and spoke with him, and he has assured him 'tis every syllable false; he received no such express.

FREEMAN

I know it. I this minute parted with my friend, who protested 95 he never sent me any such letter. Some roguish stockjobber has done it on purpose to make me lose my money, that's certain. I wish I knew who he was, I'd make him repent it — I have lost three hundred pounds by it.

TRADELOVE

What signifies your three hundred pounds† to what I have 100 lost? There's two thousand pounds to that Dutchman with the cursed long name, besides the stock I bought; the devil! I could tear my flesh. I must never show my face upon Change more, for, by my soul, I can't pay it.

FREEMAN

I am heartily sorry for't! What can I serve you in? Shall I 105 speak to the Dutch merchant and try to get you time for the payment?

TRADELOVE

Time! Adsheart! I shall never be able to look up again.

FREEMAN

I am very much concerned that I was the occasion and wish I could be an instrument of retrieving your misfortune; for my 110 own, I value it not. — Adso! A thought comes into my head, that well improved, may be of service.

TRADELOVE

Ah! There's no thought can be of any service to me, without paying the money or running away.

FREEMAN

How do you know? What do you think of my proposing 115 Mrs. Lovely to him? He is a single man, and I heard him say he had a mind to marry an English woman. Nay, more than

that, he said somebody told him, you had a pretty ward. He
wished you had bet her instead of your money.

TRADELOVE

Aye, but he'd be hanged before he'd take her instead of the   120
money; the Dutch are too covetous for that; besides, he did
not know that there were three of us, I suppose.

FREEMAN

So much the better; you may venture to give him your consent, if he'll but forgive you the wager. It is not your business
to tell him that your consent will signify nothing.   125

TRADELOVE

That's right, as you say; but will he do it, think you?

FREEMAN

I can't tell that; but I'll try what I can do with him. He has
promised me to meet me here an hour hence; I'll feel his
pulse and let you know. If I find it feasible, I'll send for you; if
not, you are at liberty to take what measures you please.   130

TRADELOVE

You must extol her beauty, double her portion, and tell him I
have the entire disposal of her, and that she can't marry without my consent; and that I am a covetous rogue and will
never part with her without a valuable consideration.

FREEMAN

Aye, aye, let me alone for a lie at a pinch.

TRADELOVE

Egad, if you can bring this to bear, Mr. Freeman, I'll make   135
you whole again; I'll pay the three hundred pounds you lost,
with all my soul.

FREEMAN

Well, I'll use my best endeavors. Where will you be?

TRADELOVE

At home; pray heaven you prosper. If I were but the sole
trustee now, I should not fear it. Who the devil would be a   140
guardian,
If when cash runs low, our coffers t'enlarge,
We can't, like other stocks, transfer our charge? (*Exit.*)

FREEMAN

Ha, ha, ha — he has it. (*Exit.*)

Scene changes to Periwinkle's house.

Enter Periwinkle on one side and footman on t' other.

FOOTMAN

A gentleman from Coventry inquires for you, sir.

PERIWINKLE

From my uncle, I warrant you, bring him up. [*Exit footman.*] This will save me the trouble, as well as the expenses of a journey.

Enter Colonel.

COLONEL

Is your name Periwinkle, sir?   5

PERIWINKLE

It is, sir.

COLONEL

I am sorry for the message I bring. My old master, whom I served these forty years, claims the sorrow due from a faithful servant to an indulgent master. (*Weeps.*)

PERIWINKLE

By this I understand, sir, my uncle, Sir Toby Periwinkle, is   10 dead.

COLONEL

He is, sir, and he has left you heir to seven hundred a year in as good abbey land as ever paid Peter-pence to Rome. I wish you long to enjoy it, but my tears will flow when I think of my benefactor. (*Weeps.*) Ah! He was a good man — he has   15 not left many of his fellows — the poor laments him sorely.

PERIWINKLE

I pray, sir, what office bore you?

COLONEL

I was his steward, sir.

PERIWINKLE

I have heard him mention you with much respect; your name is —   20

---

13 Peter-pence] annual tax paid to the papal see before the Reformation

COLONEL

Pillage, sir.

PERIWINKLE

Aye, Pillage! I do remember he called you Pillage. Pray, Mr. Pillage, when did my uncle die?

COLONEL

Monday last, at four in the morning. About two he signed this will and gave it into my hands, and strictly charged me to 25 leave Coventry the moment he expired and deliver it to you with what speed I could. I have obeyed him, sir, and there is the will. (*Gives it to Periwinkle.*)

PERIWINKLE

'Tis very well, I'll lodge it in the Commons.

COLONEL

There are two things which he forgot to insert, but charged 30 me to tell you that he desired you'd perform them as readily as if you had found them written in the will, which is to remove his corpse and bury him by his father in St. Paul, Covent Garden, and to give all his servants mourning.

PERIWINKLE

(*Aside.*) That will be a considerable charge; a pox of all mod- 35 ern fashions. [*To him.*] Well! It shall be done, Mr. Pillage; I will agree with one of death's fashion-mongers, called an undertaker, to go down and bring up the body.

COLONEL

I hope, sir, I shall have the honor to serve you in the same station I did your worthy uncle; I have not many years to stay 40 behind him and would gladly spend them in the family where I was brought up. (*Weeps.*) He was a kind and tender master to me.

PERIWINKLE

Pray don't grieve, Mr. Pillage; you shall hold your place and everything else which you held under my uncle. You make 45 me weep to see you so concerned. (*Weeps.*) He lived to a good old age — and we are all mortal.

---

34 mourning] the customary dress worn by those in mourning; in Act V Periwinkle orders black stockings and gloves

COLONEL

We are so, sir, and therefore I must beg you to sign this lease.
You'll find Sir Toby has ta'en particular notice of it in his will.
I could not get it time enough from the lawyer, or he had   50
signed it before he died. (*Gives him a paper.*)

PERIWINKLE

A lease for what?

COLONEL

I rented a hundred a year of Sir Toby upon lease, which lease
expires at Lady Day next, and I desire to renew it for twenty
years — that's all, sir.   55

PERIWINKLE

Let me see. (*Looks over the lease.*)

COLONEL

(*Aside.*) Matters go swimmingly, if nothing intervene.

PERIWINKLE

Very well. Let's see what he says in his will about it. (*Lays the
lease upon the table and looks on the will.*)

COLONEL

(*Aside.*) He's very wary, yet I fancy I shall be too cunning for   60
him.

PERIWINKLE

Ho, here it is. — The farm lying — now in possession of Samuel Pillage — suffer him to renew his lease — at the same
rent. — Very well, Mr. Pillage, I see my uncle does mention it,
and I'll perform his will. Give me the lease. (*Colonel gives it*   65
him; he looks upon it and lays it upon the table.) Pray you step to
the door and call for a pen and ink, Mr. Pillage.

COLONEL

I have pen and ink in my pocket, sir. (*Pulls out an inkhorn.*) I
never go without that.

PERIWINKLE

I think it belongs to your profession. (*He looks upon the pen*   70
while the Colonel changes the lease and lays down the contract.) I
doubt this is but a sorry pen, though it may serve to write my
name. (*Writes.*)

---

54 Lady Day] Feast of the Annunciation, 25 March; one of the four quarter days,
from which it was customary to date leases

COLONEL

(*Aside.*) Little does he think what he signs.

PERIWINKLE

There is your lease, Mr. Pillage. (*Gives him the paper.*) Now I 75
must desire you to make what haste you can down to Coventry and take care of everything, and I'll send down the undertaker for the body; do you attend it up, and whatever charge
you are at, I will repay you.

COLONEL

(*Aside.*) You have paid me already, I thank you, sir. 80

PERIWINKLE

Will you dine with me?

COLONEL

I would rather not; there are some of my neighbours which I
met as I came along, who leaves the town this afternoon, they
told me, and I should be glad of their company down.

PERIWINKLE

Well, well, I won't detain you. 85

COLONEL

(*Aside.*) I don't care how soon I am out.

PERIWINKLE

I will give orders about mourning.

COLONEL

[*Aside.*] You will have cause to mourn, when you know your
estate imaginary only.

You'll find your hopes and cares alike are vain, 90
In spite of all the caution you have ta'en,
Fortune rewards[†] the faithful lover's pain. (*Exit.*)

PERIWINKLE

Seven hundred a year! I wish he had died seventeen years ago.
What a valuable collection of rarities might I have had by this
time? I might have traveled over all the known parts of the 95
globe and made my own closet rival the Vatican at Rome.
Odso, I have a good mind to begin my travels now; — let me
see — I am but sixty! My father, grandfather, and great-
grandfather reached ninety-odd; I have almost forty years
good. Let me consider! What will seven hundred a year 100

---

96 closet] a private repository, often a cabinet, for curiosities

amount to — in — aye! in thirty years, I'll say but thirty — thirty times seven, is seven times thirty — that is — just twenty-one thousand pound — 'tis a great deal of money — I may very well reserve sixteen hundred of it for a collection of such rarities as will make my name famous to posterity. I would not die like other mortals, forgotten in a year or two, as my uncle will be. No. 105

With nature's curious works I'll raise my fame,
That men, till doomsday, may repeat my name. (*Exit.*)

Scene changes to a tavern;
Freeman and Tradelove over a bottle.

TRADELOVE

Come, Mr. Freeman, here's Mynheer Jan van Tim, Tam, Tam — I shall never think of that Dutchman's name.

FREEMAN

Mynheer Jan van Timtamtirelireletta Heer van Fainwell.

TRADELOVE

Aye, Heer van Fainwell, I never heard such a confounded name in life — here's his health, I say. (*Drinks.*) 5

FREEMAN

With all my heart.

TRADELOVE

Faith, I never expected to have found so generous a thing in a Dutchman.

FREEMAN

Oh, he has nothing of the Hollander in his temper — except an antipathy to monarchy. As soon as I told him your circum- 10 stances, he replied he would not be the ruin of any man for the world and immediately made this proposal himself. Let him take what time he will for the payment, said he; or if he'll give me his ward, I'll forgive him the debt.

---

10 antipathy to monarchy] Holland was a republic

TRADELOVE

    Well, Mr. Freeman, I can but thank you. Egad, you have made   15
a man of me again; and if ever I lay a wager more, may I rot in
a jail.†

FREEMAN

    I assure you, Mr. Tradelove, I was very much concerned be-
cause I was the occasion — though very innocently, I protest.

TRADELOVE

    I dare swear you was, Mr. Freeman.   20

Enter a fiddler.

FIDDLER

    Please to have a lesson of music or a song, gentlemen?

FREEMAN

    A song, aye, with all our hearts; have you ever a merry one?

FIDDLER

    Yes, sir, my wife and I can give you a merry dialogue.

Here is the song.

TRADELOVE

    'Tis very pretty, faith.

FREEMAN

    There's something for you to drink, friend; go, lose no time.   25

FIDDLER

    I thank you, sir. (*Exit.*)

Enter drawer and Colonel, dressed for the Dutch merchant.

COLONEL

    Ha, Mynheer Tradelove, Ik ben sorry voor your troubles,
maer Ik sal you easie maeken, Ik wil de gelt† niet hebben.

SD *dressed...merchant*] Ned Ward describes Dutch merchants on the Exchange as
"a throng of strait-laced monsters in fur, and thrum caps [made of coarse
scraps of yarn], with huge logger-heads, effeminate waists, and buttocks like a
Flanders mare, with slovenly mien and swinish looks, whose upper lips were
gracefully adorned with brown whiskers" (*London Spy* 56-57).

27-8 Ha...hebben.] Ha, Mister Tradelove, I am sorry for your troubles, but I shall
make you easy, I will not have the money.

TRADELOVE

I shall forever acknowledge the obligation, sir.

FREEMAN

But you understand upon what condition, Mr. Tradelove: 30
Mrs. Lovely.

COLONEL

Ya, de juffrow sal al te regt setten, mynheer.

TRADELOVE

With all my heart, mynheer, you shall have my consent to
marry her freely.

FREEMAN

Well then, as I am a party concerned between you, Mynheer 35
Jan van Timtamtirelireletta Heer van Fainwell shall give you a
discharge of your wager under his own hand, and you shall
give him your consent to marry Mrs. Lovely under yours;
that is the way to avoid all manner of disputes hereafter.

COLONEL

Ya, waeragtig. 40

TRADELOVE

Aye, aye, so it is, Mr. Freeman, I'll give it under mine this
minute. (*Sits down to write.*)

COLONEL

And so sal Ik. (*Sits down to write.*)

FREEMAN

So, ho, the house. (*Enter drawer.*) Bid your master come up.
[*Exit drawer.*] (*Aside.*) I'll see there be witnesses enough to the 45
bargain.

Enter Sackbut.

SACKBUT

Do you call, gentlemen?

FREEMAN

Aye, Mr. Sackbut, we shall want your hand here.

---

32 Ya...mynheer.] Yes, the young lady shall set all to right, sir.
40 Ya, waeragtig.] Yes, truly.
43 And so sal Ik.] And so shall I.

TRADELOVE

> There, mynheer, there's my consent as amply as you can de-
> sire; but you must insert your own name, for I know not how   50
> to spell it; I have left a blank for it. (*Gives the Colonel a paper.*)

COLONEL

> Ya, Ik sal dat well doen.

FREEMAN

> Now, Mr. Sackbut, you and I will witness it. (*They write.*)

COLONEL

> Daer, Mynheer Tradelove, is your discharge. (*Gives him a
> paper.*)   55

TRADELOVE

> Be pleased to witness this receipt too, gentlemen.

> *Freeman and Sackbut put their hands.*

FREEMAN

> Aye, aye, that we will.

COLONEL

> Well, mynheer, ye most meer doen, ye most myn voorspraek
> to de juffrow syn.

FREEMAN

> He means you must recommend him to the lady.   60

TRADELOVE

> That I will, and to the rest of my brother guardians.

COLONEL

> Wat, voor den duyvel, heb you meer guardians?

TRADELOVE

> Only three, mynheer.

COLONEL

> Wat donder heb ye myn betrocken mynheer? Had Ik that ge-
> woeten, Ik soude eaven met you geweest syn.   65

---

52 Ya...doen.] Yes, I shall do that well.
58-9 Well...syn.] Well, sir, you must do more, you must be my advocate to the
    young lady.
62 Wat...guardians?] What the devil, have you more guardians?
64-5 Wat...syn.] What, then have you tricked me, sir? Had I known that, I should
    have been even with you.

SACKBUT

But Mr. Tradelove is the principal, and he can do a great deal with the rest, sir.

FREEMAN

And he shall use his interest I promise you, mynheer.

TRADELOVE

I will say all that ever I can think on to recommend you, mynheer; and if you please, I'll introduce you to the lady.   70

COLONEL

Well, dat is waer. Maer ye must first spreken of myn to de juffrow and to de oudere gentlemen.

FREEMAN

Aye, that's the best way, and then I and the Heer van Fainwell will meet you there.

TRADELOVE

I will go this moment, upon honor. Your most obedient   75
humble servant. [*Aside.*] My speaking will do you little good, mynheer,† ha, ha; we have bit you, faith, ha, ha; my debt's discharged, and for the man,
He's my consent — to get her if he can. (*Exit.*)

COLONEL

Ha, ha, ha, this was a masterpiece of contrivance, Freeman.   80

FREEMAN

He hugs himself with his supposed good fortune and little thinks the luck's of our side; but come, pursue the fickle goddess while she's in the mood. Now for the Quaker.

COLONEL

That's the hardest task.
Of all the counterfeits performed by man,   85
A soldier makes the simplest puritan. (*Exit.*)†

71-2 Well...gentlemen.] Well, that is true. But you must first speak of me to the young lady and to the other gentlemen.

86 soldier...puritan.] simple — foolish; puritan — a general term commonly applied to all Dissenters. Since Quakers are pacifists and do not swear oaths, including oaths of loyalty, the transformation of soldier into Quaker is the most extreme of all.

Scene: Prim's house.

Enter Mrs. Prim and Mrs. Lovely in Quaker's dress, meeting.

MRS. PRIM

So, now I like thee, Anne. Art thou not better without thy
monstrous hoop coat and patches! If heaven should make
thee so many black spots upon thy face, would it not fright
thee, Anne?

MRS. LOVELY

If it should turn your inside outward and show all the spots of   5
your hypocrisy, 'twould fright me worse.

MRS. PRIM

My hypocrisy! I scorn thy words, Anne, I lay no baits.

MRS. LOVELY

If you did, you'd catch no fish.

MRS. PRIM

Well, well, make thy jests; but I'd have thee to know, Anne,
that I could have catched as many fish (as thou call'st them) in   10
my time, as ever thou didst with all thy fool-traps about thee.
If admirers be thy aim, thou wilt have more of them in this
dress than thy other. The men, take my word for't, are most
desirous to see what we are most careful to conceal.

MRS. LOVELY

Is that the reason of your formality, Mrs. Prim? Truth will out.   15
I ever thought, indeed, there was more design than godliness
in the pinched cap.

MRS. PRIM

Go, thou art corrupted with reading lewd plays and filthy romances, good for nothing but to lead youth into the high
road of fornication. Ah! I wish thou art not already too famil-   20
iar with the wicked ones.

---

2 hoop coat] hoop-petticoat; i.e. hoop

MRS. LOVELY

Too familiar with the wicked ones! Pray, no more of those
freedoms, madam. I am familiar with none so wicked as
yourself. How dare you talk thus to me! You, you, you un-
worthy woman you. (*Bursts into tears.*)   25

Enter Tradelove.

TRADELOVE

What, in tears, Nancy? What have you done to her, Mrs.
Prim, to make her weep?

MRS. LOVELY

Done to me! I admire I keep my senses among you; but I will
rid myself of your tyranny, if there be either law or justice to
be had; I'll force you to give me up my liberty.   30

MRS. PRIM

Thou hast more need to weep for thy sins, Anne — yea, for
thy manifold sins.

MRS. LOVELY

Don't think that I'll be still the fool which you have made
me. No, I'll wear what I please, go when and where I please,
and keep what company I think fit and not what you shall   35
direct — I will.

TRADELOVE

For my part, I do think all this very reasonable, Mrs. Lovely
— 'tis fit you should have your liberty, and for that very purpose I am come.

*Enter Mr. Periwinkle and Obadiah Prim,
with a letter in his hand.*

PERIWINKLE

I have bought some black stockings of your husband, Mrs.   40
Prim, but he tells me the glover's trade belongs to you, therefore I pray you look me out five or six dozen of mourning
gloves, such as are given at funerals, and send them to my
house.

OBADIAH PRIM

My friend Periwinkle has got a good windfall today — seven   45
hundred a year.

MRS. PRIM

I wish thee joy of it, neighbor.

TRADELOVE

What, is Sir Toby dead then?

PERIWINKLE

He is! You'll take care, Mrs. Prim?

MRS. PRIM

Yea, I will, neighbor.   50

OBADIAH PRIM

This letter recommendeth a speaker, 'tis from Aminadab
Holdfast of Bristol; peradventure he will be here this night;
therefore, Sarah, do thou take care for his reception. (*Gives her
the letter.*)

MRS. PRIM

I will obey thee. (*Exit.*)   55

OBADIAH PRIM

What art thou in the dumps for, Anne?

TRADELOVE

We must marry her, Mr. Prim.

OBADIAH PRIM

Why truly, if we could find a husband worth having, I should
be as glad to see her married as thou wouldst, neighbor.

PERIWINKLE

Well said, there are but few worth having.   60

TRADELOVE

I can recommend you a man now, that I think you can none
of you have an objection to!†

Enter Sir Philip Modelove.

PERIWINKLE

You recommend! Nay, whenever she marries, I'll recommend the husband.

SIR PHILIP

What, must it be a whale or a rhinoceros,† Mr. Periwinkle,   65
ha, ha ha? Mr. Tradelove, I have a bill upon you (*gives him a
paper*) and have been seeking for you all over the town.

---

51 speaker] minister
66 bill] bill of exchange, a written order for payment of a specified amount of
money to a designated person

TRADELOVE

I'll accept it, Sir Philip, and pay it when due.

PERIWINKLE

He shall be none of the fops at your end of the town, with
full perukes and empty skulls, nor yet none of your trading   70
gentry, who puzzle the heralds to find arms for their coaches.
No, he shall be a man famous for travels, solidity, and curiosity, one who has searched into the profundity of nature; when
heaven shall direct such a one, he shall have my consent, because it may turn to the benefit of mankind.   75

MRS. LOVELY

The benefit of mankind! What, would you anatomize me?

SIR PHILIP

Aye, aye, madam, he would dissect[†] you.

TRADELOVE

Or pore over you through a microscope to see how your
blood circulates from the crown of your head to the sole of
your foot, ha, ha! But I have a husband for you, a man that   80
knows how to improve your fortune; one that trades to the
four corners of the globe.

MRS. LOVELY

And would send me for a venture perhaps.

TRADELOVE

One that will dress you in all the pride of Europe, Asia, Af-
rica, and America — a Dutch merchant, my girl!   85

SIR PHILIP

A Dutchman! Ha, ha, there's a husband for a fine lady — Ya,
juffrow, will you met myn slapen — ha, ha; he'll learn you to
talk the language of the hogs, madam, ha, ha.

TRADELOVE

He'll learn you that one merchant is of more service to a nation than fifty coxcombs. The Dutch know the trading inter-   90
est to be of more benefit to the state than the landed.

---

70 perukes] wigs
78-9 microscope...circulates] research on circulation was advanced by the use of
   the microscope, which allowed observation of the capillaries
86-7 Ya...slappen] Yes, young lady, will you sleep with me?
88 language of the hogs] the Dutch language was satirically described as sounding
   like hogs grunting (see Ward, *London Spy* 57)

SIR PHILIP

But what is either interest to a lady?

TRADELOVE

'Tis the merchant makes the belle. How would the ladies
sparkle in the box without the merchant? The Indian dia-
monds! The French brocade! The Italian fan! The Flanders   95
lace! The fine Dutch holland! How would they vent their
scandal over their tea-tables? And where would you beaus
have champagne to toast your mistresses, were it not for the
merchant?

OBADIAH PRIM

Verily, neighbor Tradelove, thou dost waste thy breath about   100
nothing. All that thou hast said tendeth only to debauch
youth and fill their heads with the pride and luxury of this
world. The merchant is a very great friend to Satan, and sen-
deth as many to his dominions as the pope.

PERIWINKLE

Right, I say knowledge makes the man.   105

OBADIAH PRIM

Yea, but not thy kind of knowledge — it is the knowledge of
Truth. Search thou for the light within, and not for baubles,
Friend.

MRS. LOVELY

Ah, study your country's good, Mr. Periwinkle, and not her
insects. Rid you of your homebred monsters before you fetch   110
any from abroad. I dare swear you have maggots enough in
your own brain to stock all the virtuosos[†] in Europe with
butterflies.

SIR PHILIP

By my soul, Miss Nancy's a wit.

OBADIAH PRIM

That is more than she can say by thee, friend. Look ye, it is in   115
vain to talk; when I meet a man worthy of her, she shall have
my leave to marry him.

---

94 the box] at the theater
96 holland] a linen fabric
111 maggots] fig. whimsical fancies

MRS. LOVELY

Provided he be one of the faithful. (*Aside.*) Was there ever such a swarm of caterpillars to blast the hopes of a woman! [*Aloud.*] Know this, that you contend in vain: I'll have no 120 husband of your choosing, nor shall you lord it over me long. I'll try the power of an English senate. Orphans have been redressed and wills set aside, and none did ever deserve their pity more. [*Aside.*] Oh Fainwell! Where are thy promises to free me from these vermin? Alas! The task was more difficult 125 than he imagined!

A harder task than what the poets tell
Of yore, the fair Andromeda† befell;
She but one monster feared, I've four to fear,
And see no Perseus,† no deliv'rer near. (*Exit.*) 130

Enter servant and whispers to Prim.

SERVANT

One Simon Pure inquireth for thee.

PERIWINKLE

The woman is mad. (*Exit.*)

SIR PHILIP

So are you all, in my opinion. (*Exit.*)

OBADIAH PRIM

Friend Tradelove, business requireth my presence.

TRADELOVE

Oh, I shan't trouble you. [*Aside.*] Pox take him for an unman- 135 nerly dog. However, I have kept my word with my Dutchman, and will introduce him too for all you. (*Exit.*)

Enter Colonel in a Quaker's habit.

OBADIAH PRIM

Friend Pure, thou art welcome; how is it with Friend Holdfast, and all Friends in Bristol? Timothy Littlewit, John Slenderbrain, and Christopher Keepfaith? 140

128-30 Andromeda...Perseus] the hero Perseus rescued Andromeda from a sea-monster and was rewarded by marriage to her

COLONEL

(*Aside.*) A goodly company! [*To him.*] They are all in health, I
thank thee for them.

OBADIAH PRIM

Friend Holdfast writes me word that thou camest lately from
Pennsylvania; how do all Friends there?

COLONEL

(*Aside.*) What the devil shall I say? I know just as much of   145
Pennsylvania as I do of Bristol.

OBADIAH PRIM

Do they thrive?

COLONEL

Yea, Friend, the blessing of their good works fall upon them.

Enter Mrs. Prim and Mrs. Lovely.

OBADIAH PRIM

Sarah, know our Friend Pure.

MRS. PRIM

Thou art welcome.   150

He salutes her.

COLONEL

(*Aside.*) Here comes the sum of all my wishes. How charming she appears, even in that disguise.

OBADIAH PRIM

Why dost thou consider the maiden so intentively, Friend?

COLONEL

I will tell thee. About four days ago I saw a vision — this very
maiden, but in vain attire, standing on a precipice[†]; and heard   155
a voice, which called me by my name and bade me put forth
my hand and save her from the pit. I did so, and methought
the damosel grew to my side.

SD *salutes*] kisses
153 intentively] earnestly, intently
158 damosel] arch. damsel; archaic spelling contributes to the parody of prophetic
    speech throughout this scene

MRS. PRIM

What can that portend?

OBADIAH PRIM

The damosel's conversion — I am persuaded.   160

MRS. LOVELY

(*Aside.*) That's false I'm sure.

OBADIAH PRIM

Wilt thou use the means, Friend Pure?

COLONEL

Means! What means? Is she not thy daughter, and already one
of the faithful?

MRS. PRIM

No, alas! She's one of the ungodly.   165

OBADIAH PRIM

Pray thee mind what this good man will say unto thee; he
will teach thee the way that thou shouldest walk, Anne.

MRS. LOVELY

I know my way without his instructions. I hoped to have
been quiet, when once I had put on your odious formality
here.   170

COLONEL

Then thou wearest it out of compulsion, not choice, Friend?

MRS. LOVELY

Thou art in the right of it, Friend.

MRS. PRIM

Art not thou ashamed to mimic the good man? Ah! Thou art
a stubborn girl.

COLONEL

Mind her not; she hurteth not me. If thou wilt leave her   175
alone with me, I will discuss some few points with her that
may, perchance, soften her stubborness and melt her into
compliance.

OBADIAH PRIM

Content, I pray thee put it home to her. Come, Sarah, let us
leave the good man with her.   180

MRS. LOVELY

(*Catching hold of Prim; he breaks loose and exit* [*with Mrs.
Prim*].) What do you mean — to leave me with this old en-
thusiastical canter? Don't think, because I complied with
your formality, to impose your ridiculous doctrine upon me.

COLONEL

I pray thee, young woman, moderate thy passion.   185

MRS. LOVELY

I pray thee, walk after thy leader; you will but lose your labor
upon me. — These wretches will certainly make me mad.

COLONEL

I am of another opinion; the spirit telleth me that I shall convert thee, Anne.

MRS. LOVELY

'Tis a lying spirit; don't believe it.   190

COLONEL

Say'st thou so? Why then thou shalt convert me, my angel.
(Catching her in his arms.)

MRS. LOVELY

(Shrieks.) Ah! Monster, hold off, or I'll tear thy eyes out.

COLONEL

Hush! For heaven's sake — dost thou know me? I am Fainwell.   195

MRS. LOVELY

Fainwell!

Enter old Prim.

(Aside.) Oh I'm undone, Prim here. I wish with all my soul I
had been dumb.

OBADIAH PRIM

What is the matter? Why didst thou shriek out, Anne?

MRS. LOVELY

Shriek out! I'll shriek and shriek again, cry murder, thieves,   200
or anything to drown the noise of that eternal babbler, if you
leave me with him any longer.

OBADIAH PRIM

Was that all? Fie, fie, Anne.

COLONEL

No matter, I'll bring down her stomach, I'll warrant thee —
leave us, I pray thee.   205

---

204 stomach] temper, disposition

OBADIAH PRIM

Fare thee well. (*Exit.*)

COLONEL

(*Embraces her.*) My charming, lovely woman.

MRS. LOVELY

What means thou by this disguise, Fainwell?

COLONEL

To set thee free, if thou wilt perform thy promise.

MRS. LOVELY

Make me mistress of my fortune and make thy own condi- 210
tions.

COLONEL

This night shall answer all thy wishes. See here, I have the
consent of three of thy guardians already, and doubt not but
Prim shall make the fourth.

Prim listening.

OBADIAH PRIM

(*Aside*) I would gladly hear what argument the good man 215
useth to bend her.

MRS. LOVELY

Thy words give me new life, methinks.

OBADIAH PRIM

What do I hear?

MRS. LOVELY

Thou best of men, heaven meant to bless me sure, when I
first saw thee. 220

OBADIAH PRIM

He hath mollified her. Oh wonderful conversion!

COLONEL

Ha! Prim listening. [*Aside to Mrs. Lovely.*] No more, my love,
we are observed; seem to be edified and give 'em hopes that
thou wilt turn Quaker, and leave the rest to me. (*Aloud.*) I am
glad to find that thou art touched with what I said unto thee, 225
Anne; another time I will explain the other article to thee; in
the meanwhile be thou dutiful to our Friend Prim.

MRS. LOVELY

I shall obey thee in everything.

Enter old Prim.

OBADIAH PRIM

Oh what a prodigious change is here! Thou hast wrought a miracle, Friend! Anne, how dost thou like the doctrine he 230 hath preached?

MRS. LOVELY

So well, that I could talk to him forever, methinks. I am ashamed of my former folly and ask your pardon, Mr. Prim.

COLONEL

Enough, enough that thou art sorry; he is no pope, Anne.

OBADIAH PRIM

Verily, thou dost rejoice me exceedingly, friend; will it please 235 thee to walk into the next room and refresh thyself? Come, take the maiden by the hand.

COLONEL

We will follow thee.

Enter servant.

SERVANT

There is another Simon Pure inquireth for thee, master.

COLONEL

(*Aside.*) The devil there is. 240

OBADIAH PRIM

Another Simon Pure? I do not know him, is he any relation of thine?

COLONEL

No, Friend, I know him not. (*Aside.*) Pox take him, I wish he were in Pennsylvania again, with all my blood.

MRS. LOVELY

(*Aside.*) What shall I do? 245

OBADIAH PRIM

Bring him up.

COLONEL

[*Aside.*] Humph! Then one of us must go down, that's certain. Now impudence assist me.

Enter Simon Pure.

OBADIAH PRIM

What is thy will with me, Friend?

SIMON PURE

Didst thou not receive a letter from Aminadab Holdfast of   250
Bristol concerning one Simon Pure?

OBADIAH PRIM

Yea, and Simon Pure is already here, Friend.

COLONEL

(*Aside.*) And Simon Pure will stay here, Friend, if possible.

SIMON PURE

That's an untruth, for I am he.

COLONEL

Take thou heed, Friend, what thou dost say; I do affirm that I   255
am Simon Pure.

SIMON PURE

Thy name may be Pure, Friend, but not that Pure.

COLONEL

Yea, that Pure which my good Friend Aminadab Holdfast
wrote to my Friend Prim about, the same Simon Pure that
came from Pennsylvania and sojourned in Bristol eleven   260
days; thou wouldst not take my name from me, wouldst
thou? (*Aside.*) Till I have done with it.

SIMON PURE

Thy name! I am astonished.

COLONEL

At what? At thy own assurance?

Going up to him; Simon Pure starts back.

SIMON PURE

Avant, Sathan; approach me not; I defy thee and all thy   265
works.

MRS. LOVELY

(*Aside.*) Oh, he'll out-cant him. Undone, undone forever.

---

265 *Avant Sathan*] arch. sp. Avaunt [begone] Satan

COLONEL

>Hark thee, Friend, thy sham will not take. Don't exert thy voice; thou art too well acquainted with Sathan to start at him, thou wicked reprobate. What can thy design be here? 270

Enter servant, and gives Prim a letter.

OBADIAH PRIM

>One of these must be a counterfeit, but which I cannot say.

COLONEL

>(*Aside.*) What can that letter be?

SIMON PURE

>Thou must be the devil, Friend, that's certain, for no human power can stock so great a falsehood.

OBADIAH PRIM

>This letter sayeth that thou art better acquainted with that 275 prince of darkness than any here. Read that, I pray thee, Simon. (*Gives it the Colonel.*)

COLONEL

>[*Aside.*] 'Tis Freeman's hand. (*Reads.*) There is a design formed to rob your house this night and cut your throat, and for that purpose there is a man disguised like a Quaker, who 280 is to pass for one Simon Pure; the gang whereof I am one, though now resolved to rob no more, has been at Bristol; one of them came up in the coach with the Quaker, whose name he hath taken, and from what he gathered from him, formed that design, and did not doubt but he should impose so far 285 upon you as to make you turn out the real Simon Pure and keep him with you. Make the right use of this. Adieu. (*Aside.*) Excellent well!

OBADIAH PRIM

>(*To Simon Pure.*) Dost thou hear this?

SIMON PURE

>Yea, but it moveth me not; that, doubtless, is the impostor. 290 (*Pointing at the Colonel.*)

COLONEL

Ah! Thou wicked one — now I consider thy face I remember thou didst come up in the leathern convenience with me — thou hadst a black bob wig on, and a brown camblet coat with brass buttons — canst thou deny it, ha?   295

SIMON PURE

Yea, I can, and with a safe conscience too, Friend.

OBADIAH PRIM

Verily, Friend, thou art the most impudent villain I ever saw.

MRS. LOVELY

(*Aside*.) Nay then, I'll have a fling at him too. [*Aloud*.] I remember the face of this fellow at Bath. Aye, this is he that picked my Lady Raffle's pocket upon the Grove. Don't you   300
remember that the mob pumped you, Friend? This is the most notorious rogue.

SIMON PURE

What doth provoke thee to seek my life? Thou wilt not hang me, wilt thou, wrongfully?

OBADIAH PRIM

She will do thee no hurt, nor thou shalt do me none; there-   305
fore get thee about thy business, Friend, and leave thy wicked course of life, or thou may'st not come off so favorably everywhere.

COLONEL

Go, Friend, I would advise thee, and tempt thy fate no more.

SIMON PURE

Yea, I will go, but it shall be to thy confusion; for I shall clear   310
myself. I will return with some proofs that shall convince thee, Obadiah, that thou art highly imposed upon. (*Exit.*)

COLONEL

(*Aside*.) Then here will be no staying for me, that's certain. What the devil shall I do?

---

293 leathern convenience] coach; a parody of Quaker literalness in the interest of strict truthfulness

294 camblet] a light cloth of mixed silk and wool

300 the Grove] the Orange Grove, a public walk planted with trees named for a column honoring William of Orange

301 pumped] put under a stream of water from a pump, for punishment

303-4 hang me] theft was punishable by death

OBADIAH PRIM

What monstrous works of iniquity are there in this world,   315
Simon!

COLONEL

Yea, the age is full of vice. (*Aside.*) Z'death, I am so confounded, I know not what to say.

OBADIAH PRIM

Thou art disordered, Friend — art thou not well?

COLONEL

My spirit is greatly troubled, and something telleth me, that   320
though I have wrought a good work in converting this
maiden, this tender maiden, yet my labor will be in vain; for
the evil spirit fighteth against her; and I see, yea I see with the
eyes of my inward man, that Sathan will rebuffet her again,
whenever I withdraw myself from her; and she will, yea this   325
very damosel will return again to that abomination from
whence I have retrieved her, as if it were, yea, as if it were out
of the jaws of the fiend — hum —

OBADIAH PRIM

Good lack! Thinkest thou so?

MRS. LOVELY

(*Aside.*) I must second him. [*Aloud.*] What meaneth this   330
struggling within me? I feel the spirit resisting the vanities of
this world, but the flesh is rebellious, yea the flesh — I greatly
fear the flesh and the weakness thereof — hum —

OBADIAH PRIM

The maid is inspired.

COLONEL

Behold, her light begins to shine forth. (*Aside.*) Excellent   335
woman!

MRS. LOVELY

This good man hath spoken comfort unto me, yea comfort, I
say; because the words which he hath breathed into my outward ears are gone through and fixed in mine heart, yea verily in mine heart, I say — and I feel the spirit doth love him   340
exceedingly, hum —

---

328 hum] a parody of the sobbing or groaning that punctuated Quaker preaching,
a sign of spiritual struggle and inspiration (Frost 36; Bauman 127)

COLONEL

(*Aside.*) She acts it to the life.

OBADIAH PRIM

Prodigious! The damosel is filled with the spirit, Sarah!

Enter Mrs. Prim.

MRS. PRIM

I am greatly rejoiced to see such a change in our beloved
Anne. I came to tell thee that supper stayeth for thee.   345

COLONEL

I am not disposed for thy food — my spirit longeth for more
delicious meat; fain would I redeem this maiden from the
tribe of sinners and break those cords asunder wherewith she
is bound — hum —

MRS. LOVELY

Something whispers in my ears, methinks, that I must be sub-   350
ject to the will of this good man, and from him only must
hope for consolation — hum — it also telleth me that I am a
chosen vessel to raise up seed to the faithful, and that thou
must consent that we two be one flesh according to the word
— hum —   355

OBADIAH PRIM

What a revelation is here? This is certainly part of thy vision,
Friend, this is the maiden's growing to thy side. Ah! With
what willingness should I give thee my consent, could I give
thee her fortune too, but thou wilt never get the consent of
the wicked ones.   360

COLONEL

(*Aside.*) I wish I was as sure of yours.

OBADIAH PRIM

My soul rejoiceth, yea, it rejoiceth, I say, to find the spirit
within thee; for lo, it moveth thee with natural agitation —
yea, with natural agitation, I say again, and stirreth up the
seeds of thy virgin inclination towards this good man — yea,   365
it stirreth, as one may say — yea verily, I say it stirreth up thy
inclination — yea, as one would stir a pudding.

MRS. LOVELY

I see, I see! The spirit guiding of thy hand, good Obadiah
Prim, and now behold thou art signing thy consent; and now

I see myself within thy arms, my friend and brother, yea, I am 370
become bone of thy bone and flesh of thy flesh. (*Embraces
him.*) Hum —

COLONEL

(*Aside.*) Admirably performed. [*Aloud.*] And I will take thee
in all spiritual love for an helpmate,[†] yea, for the wife of my
bosom; and now, methinks, I feel a longing, yea, a longing, I 375
say, for the consummation of thy love, hum — yea, I do long
exceedingly.

MRS. LOVELY

And verily, verily my spirit feeleth the same longing.

MRS. PRIM

The spirit hath greatly moved them both. Friend Prim, thou
must consent; there is no resisting of the spirit. 380

OBADIAH PRIM

Yea, the light within showeth me that I shall fight a good
fight and wrestle through those reprobate fiends, thy other
guardians — yea, I perceive the spirit will hedge thee into the
flock of the righteous. Thou art a chosen lamb — yea, a chosen lamb, and I will not push thee back — no, I will not, I say 385
— no, thou shalt leap-a, and frisk-a, and skip-a, and bound,
and bound, I say — yea, bound within the fold of the righteous — yea, even within thy fold, my brother. Fetch me the
pen and ink, Sarah — and my hand shall confess its obedi-
ence to the spirit. 390

COLONEL

[*Aside.*] I wish it were over.

Enter Mrs. Prim with pen and ink.

MRS. LOVELY

(*Aside.*) I tremble lest[†] this Quaking rogue should return and
spoil all.

OBADIAH PRIM

Here, Friend, do thou write what the spirit prompteth and I
will sign it. 395

Colonel sits down [and writes].

MRS. PRIM

Verily, Anne, it greatly rejoiceth me, to see thee reformed from that original wickedness wherein I found thee.

MRS. LOVELY

I do believe thou art, and I thank thee.

COLONEL

(*Reads.*) This is to certify all whom it may concern, that I do freely give up all my right and title in Anne Lovely to Simon Pure, and my full consent that she shall become his wife according to the form of marriage. Witness my hand.

OBADIAH PRIM

That is enough — give me the pen. (*Signs it.*)

Enter Betty running to Mrs. Lovely.

BETTY

Oh! Madam, madam, here's the Quaking man again; he has brought a coachman and two or three more.

MRS. LOVELY

(*Aside to Colonel.*) Ruined past redemption.

COLONEL

[*Aside to her.*] No, no, one minute sooner had spoiled all, but now — (*Going up to Prim hastily.*) Here is company coming, Friend, give me the paper.

OBADIAH PRIM

Here it is, Simon, and I wish thee happy with the maiden.

MRS. LOVELY

'Tis done, and now, devil do thy worst.

Enter Simon Pure and coachman, &c.

SIMON PURE

Look thee, Friend, I have brought these people to satisfy thee that I am not that impostor which thou didst[†] take me for; this is the man which did drive the leathern conveniency that brought me from Bristol, and this is —

COLONEL

Look ye, Friend, to save the court the trouble of examining witnesses, I plead guilty, ha, ha!

OBADIAH PRIM

How's this? Is not thy name Pure, then?

COLONEL

No really, sir, I only made bold with this gentleman's name; but I here give it up safe and sound; it has done the business 420 which I had occasion for, and now I intend to wear my own, which shall be at his service upon the same occasion at any time, ha, ha, ha!

SIMON PURE

Oh! The wickedness of this age.

COACHMAN

Then you have no farther need of us, sir. (*Exit*.) 425

COLONEL

No, honest man, you may go about your business.

OBADIAH PRIM

I am struck dumb with thy impudence, Anne; thou hast deceived me and perchance undone thyself.

MRS. PRIM

Thou art a dissembling baggage, and shame will overtake thee. (*Exit*.) 430

SIMON PURE

I am grieved to see thy wife so much troubled; I will follow and console her. (*Exit*.)

Enter servant.

SERVANT

Thy brother guardians inquireth for thee; there is another man with them.

MRS. LOVELY

(*To the Colonel*.) Who can that other man be? 435

COLONEL

'Tis one Freeman, a friend of mine, whom I ordered to bring the rest of thy guardians here.

Enter Sir Philip, Tradelove, Periwinkle, and Freeman.

---

429 baggage] a good-for-nothing woman

FREEMAN

(*To the Colonel.*) Is all safe? Did[†] my letter do you service?

COLONEL

(*Aside.*) All! All's safe; ample service.

SIR PHILIP

Miss Nancy, how dost do, child?   440

MRS. LOVELY

Don't call me miss, Friend Philip, my name is Anne, thou knowest.

SIR PHILIP

What, is the girl metamorphosed?

MRS. LOVELY

I wish thou wert so metamorphosed. Ah! Philip, throw off that gaudy attire and wear the clothes becoming of thy age.   445

OBADIAH PRIM

(*Aside.*) I am ashamed to see these men.

SIR PHILIP

My age! The woman is possessed.

COLONEL

No, thou art possessed rather, Friend.

TRADELOVE

Hark ye, Mrs. Lovely, one word with you. (*Takes hold of her hand.*)   450

COLONEL

This maiden is my wife, thanks to Friend Prim, and thou hast no business with her. (*Takes her from him.*)

TRADELOVE

His wife! Hark ye, Mr. Freeman.

PERIWINKLE

Why, you have made a very fine piece of work of it, Mr. Prim.   455

SIR PHILIP

Married to a Quaker! Thou art a fine fellow to be left guardian to an orphan, truly — there's a husband for a young lady!

COLONEL

When I have put on my beau clothes, Sir Philip, you'll like me better.

SIR PHILIP

Thou wilt make a very scurvy beau, Friend.   460

COLONEL

I believe I can prove it under your hand that you thought me
a very fine gentleman in the park today, about thirty-six minutes after eleven; will you take a pinch, Sir Philip — out of
the finest snuffbox you ever saw. (*Offers him snuff.*)

SIR PHILIP

Ha, ha, ha! I am overjoyed, faith I am, if thou be'st that gen-   465
tleman. I own I did give my consent to the gentleman I
brought here today, but if this is he I can't be positive.

OBADIAH PRIM

Canst thou not. Now I think thou art a fine fellow to be left
guardian to an orphan. Thou shallow-brained shuttlecock, he
may be a pickpocket for aught thou dost know.   470

PERIWINKLE

You would have been two rare fellows to have been trusted
with the sole management of her fortune, would ye not,
think ye? But Mr. Tradelove and myself shall take care of her
portion.

TRADELOVE

Aye, aye, so we will. Did not you tell me the Dutch merchant   475
desired me to meet him here,[†] Mr. Freeman?

FREEMAN

I did so, and I am sure he will be here, if you have a little patience.

COLONEL

What, is Mr. Tradelove impatient? Nay then, ik ben gereet
veor you, heb ye Jan van Timtamtirelireletta Heer van Fain-   480
well vergeeten?

TRADELOVE

Oh! Pox of the name! What, have you tricked me too, Mr.
Freeman?

COLONEL

Tricked, Mr. Tradelove! Did I not give you two thousand
pound for your consent fairly? And now do you tell a gentle-   485
man[†] that he has tricked you?

479-81 ik...vergeeten?] I am ready for you, have you Jan...forgotten?

PERIWINKLE

So, so, you are a pretty guardian, faith, sell your charge; what, did you look upon her as part of your stock?

OBADIAH PRIM

Ha, ha, ha! I am glad thy knavery is found out however. I confess the maiden overreached me, and no sinister end at all. 490

PERIWINKLE

Aye, aye, one thing or another overreached you all, but I'll take care he shall never finger a penny of her money, I warrant you. Overreached, quoth'a? Why I might have been overreached too, if I had had no more wit. I don't know but this very fellow may be him that was directed to me from 495 Grand Cairo today. Ha, ha, ha.

COLONEL

The very same, sir.

PERIWINKLE

Are you so, sir, but your trick would not pass upon me.

COLONEL

No, as you say, at that time it did not, that was not my lucky hour; but hark ye, sir, I must let you into one secret — you 500 may keep honest John Tradescant's coat on, for your uncle, Sir Toby Periwinkle, is not dead — so the charge of mourning will be saved, ha, ha — don't you remember Mr. Pillage, your uncle's steward, ha, ha, ha?

PERIWINKLE

Not dead! I begin to fear I am tricked too. 505

COLONEL

Don't you remember the signing of a lease, Mr. Periwinkle?

PERIWINKLE

Well, and what signifies that lease, if my uncle is not dead? Ha! I am sure it was a lease I signed.

COLONEL

Aye, but it was a lease for life, sir, and of this† beautiful tenement, I thank you. (*Taking hold of Mrs. Lovely.*) 510

OMNES

Ha, ha, ha, neighbor's fare!

509-10 tenement] residence; fig. the body, as the home of the soul
OMNES] all

FREEMAN

So then, I find you are all tricked, ha, ha!

PERIWINKLE

I am certain I read as plain a lease as ever I read in my life.

COLONEL

You read a lease I grant you, but you signed this contract. (*Showing a paper.*) 515

PERIWINKLE

How durst you put this trick upon me, Mr. Freeman, did you not tell me my uncle was dying?

FREEMAN

And would tell you twice as much to serve my friend, ha, ha.

SIR PHILIP

What, the learned, famous Mr. Periwinkle choused too? Ha, ha, ha! I shall die with laughing, ha, ha, ha. 520

OBADIAH PRIM

It had been well if her father had left her to wiser heads than thine and mine, friend, ha, ha.

TRADELOVE

Well, since you have outwitted us all, pray you, what and who are you, sir?

SIR PHILIP

Sir, the gentleman is a fine gentleman. I am glad you have got 525 a person, madam, who understands dress and good breeding. I was resolved she should have a husband of my choosing.

OBADIAH PRIM

I am sorry the maiden is fallen into such hands.

TRADELOVE

A beau! Nay then, she is finely helped up.

MRS. LOVELY

Why, beaus are great encouragers of trade, sir, ha, ha! 530

COLONEL

Look ye, gentlemen, I am the person who† can give the best account of myself, and I must beg† Sir Philip's pardon, when I tell him that I have as much aversion to what he calls† dress and breeding as I have to the enemies of my religion. I have had the honor to serve his majesty, and headed a regiment of 535 the bravest fellows that ever pushed bayonet in the throat of a Frenchman; and, notwithstanding the fortune this lady brings

me, whenever my country wants my aid, this sword and arm
are at her service.
And now, my fair, if you'll but deign to smile,
I meet a recompense for all my toil: 540
Love and religion ne'er admit restraint,
Force makes many a sinner, not one saint;
Still free as air the active mind does rove,
And searches proper objects for its love;
But that once fixed, 'tis past the power of art,   545
To chase the dear ideas from the heart:
'Tis liberty of choice that sweetens life,
Makes the glad husband, and the happy wife.

EPILOGUE[†]

*Written by Mr. Sewell and
Spoken by Mrs. Bullock*

What new strange ways our modern beaus devise!
What trials of love-skill to gain the prize!
The heathen gods, who never mattered rapes,
Scarce wore such strange variety of shapes:
The devil take their odious barren skulls,   5
To court in form of snakes and filthy bulls.
Old Jove once nicked it, I am told,
In a whole lapful of true standard gold;
How must his godship then fair Danaë[†] warm?
In trucking ware for ware there is no harm.   10
Well, after all — that money has a charm:

Mr. Sewell] George Sewell (d. 1726). A physician, hack writer, and political
    controversialist, who wrote for the Tories up to c. 1715 and then for the
    Whigs.

6 filthy bulls] Jupiter carried off Europa while disguised as a bull

7 nicked it] hit the mark; but "to nick" also had the connotations to cheat, to
    catch unawares, to copulate

9 Danaë] Jupiter reached Danaë, whose father had imprisoned her in a tower, in
    the form of a shower of gold; the allusion is to prostitution

10 trucking...ware] trucking — bartering, but also having sexual intercourse with;
    ware — merchandise, but also, the genitals

But now indeed that stale invention's past;
Besides, you know, that guineas fall so fast,
Poor nymph must come to pocket piece at last.
Old Harry's face, or good Queen Bess's ruff,   15
Not that I'd take 'em — may do well enough;
No — my ambitious spirit's far above
Those little tricks of mercenary love.
That man be mine, who, like the Colonel here,
Can top his character in every sphere;   20
Who can a thousand ways employ his wit,
Out-promise statesmen, and out-cheat a cit;
Beyond the colors of a traveler paint,
And cant, and ogle too — beyond a saint.
The last disguise most pleased me, I confess,   25
There's something tempting in the preaching dress,
And pleased me more than once a dame of note,
Who loved her husband in his footman's coat.
To see one eye in wanton motions played,
Th'other to the heavenly regions strayed,   30
As if it for its fellow's frailties prayed.
But yet I hope, for all that I have said,
To find my spouse a man of war in bed.

FINIS

---

13 guineas...fast] due to devaluation
14 nymph] prostitute (coll.)
14 pocket piece] a piece of money carried as a lucky coin, usually damaged or not
   current
15 Old Harry's face...ruff] old coins from the reigns of Henry VIII or Elizabeth I,
   bearing the image of the sovereign's face
20 top his character] play his role to perfection
22 cit] citizen; pejorative term for an inhabitant of the City

TEXTUAL NOTES

Dedication

28. ere] D2; e'er D1.

76. CENTLIVRE] Cent-Livre D1, D2.

Prologue

4. Molière] Moliere D2; Moleire D1.

11. rode] rid D1, D2

Dramatis Personae

7. *senior*] sen. D1

8. Obadiah] Obediah D1; silently changed throughout

9. *Christopher*] Chr. D1

Title WIFE] D2; WIFE, &c. D1

I.i. 39. sent] D1a, D2; Tent D1b

I.i. 80. guardians] D2; Guaadians D1

I.ii. 68. thine] followed by: *The End of the First ACT.* D1, D2

II.i. 45. Coxcombs] D2; Coxcomb's D1

II.i. 76. and] D2; and and D1

II.ii. 21. prudery] Prudry D1, D2

II.ii. 22. Prudery] Prudry D1, D2

II.ii. 76. sect] Sex D1, D2

II.ii. 85. lest] D2; least D1

II.ii. 88. filthily] D2; fiithily D1

II.ii. 98. *Exit [servant].*] Exit follows the servant's line D1, D2

II.ii. 129. fall] D2; falls D1

II.ii. 207. hit.] followed by: *End of the Second ACT.* D1, D2

III.i. 75. hippopotamus] *Hippotamus* D1, D2

III.i. 90. Descartes] D2; *Discartes* D1

III.i. 91. Descartes] D2; *Discartes* D1

III.i. 123. Carribean] *Carribian* D1, D2

III.i. 215. cockatoo] *Cockatoor* D1, D2

III.i. 248. possess] D2; profess D1

III.i. 283. *pagod*] D2; *paegod* D1

III.i. 360. way.] followed by: *The End of the Third ACT.* D1; *End of the Third Act.* D2

IV.i. 6. three-fourths] 3 *Fourths* D1, D2

IV.i. 15. come] D2; comes D1

IV.i. 42   *All together*] D2; *Altogether* D1
IV.i. 43.   five thousand pounds] 5000l. D1, D2
IV.i. 45.   all together] D2; altogether D1
IV.i. 94.   gelt] D2; Celt D1
IV.i. 95.   wager] this line and the following are assigned to Tradelove,
             with the speech prefix repeated before each line D1, D2
IV.i. 103. Timtamtirelireletta] *Timtamtirelereletta* D1, D2
IV.i. 113. Humphrey] D2; *Humphry* D1
IV.i. 114. Humphrey] *Humphry* D1; Humprey D2
IV.i. 26.   Pennsylvania] *Pensilvania* D1, D2 throughout
IV.ii. 42.   Sackbut] *Sackbutt* D1, D2
IV.ii. 48.   Periwinkle] D2; *Priwinkle* D1
IV.ii. 100. three hundred pounds] 300l. D1, D2
IV.iii. 92. rewards] D1b, D2; *reward* D1a
IV.iv. 17.   jail] Goal D1, D2
IV.iv. 28.   de gelt] degelt D1, D2
IV.iv. 77.   mynheer] Minheer D1, D2
IV.iv. 86.   *Exit.*] followed by: *End of the Fourth ACT.* D1; *The End of the Fourth Act.* D2
V.i.   62.   to!] D2; too! D1
V.i.   65.   rhinoceros] Renoseris D1; Rinoceros D2
V.i.   77.   dissect] D2; desect D1
V.i.   112. virtuosos] *Virtuoso's* D1, D2
V.i.   128. Andromeda] Andromade D1; Andromada D2
V.i.   130. Perseus] D2; Persius D1
V.i.   155. precipice] D2; Precipiece D1
V.i.   374. helpmate] D2; Helpmete D1
V.i.   392. lest] D2; least D1
V.i.   413. didst] didest D1, D2
V.i.   438. safe? Did] D2; safe did D1
V.i.   476. here] D2, her D1
V.i.   486. gentleman] Gentlemen D1, D2
V.i.   509. this] D2; his D1
V.i.   531. who] D2; missing D1
V.i.   532. beg] D2; missing D1
V.i.   533. calls] D2; call's D1

Epilogue
Title   EPILOGUE] at the end of Act V D2; following the prologue D1
      9   Danaë] D2; Daëne D1

Appendix: Selected Documents

A: Biography

1. From Giles Jacob, "Mrs. Susanna Cent Livre," *The Poetical Register: or, the Lives and Characters of the English Dramatic Poets, with an Account of Their Writings* (London: 1719) 31-32.

This Gentlewoman, now living, is Daughter of one Mr. *Freeman*, late of *Holbeach*, in *Lincolnshire*, who married a Daughter of Mr. *Marham*, a Gentleman of good Estate at *Lynn Regis*, in the County of *Norfolk*. There was formerly an Estate in the Family of her Father; but he being a Dissenter, and a zealous Parliamentarian, was so very much persecuted at the Restoration, that he was necessitated to fly into *Ireland*, and his Estate was confiscated: Nor was the Family of her Mother free from the Severities of those Times, they being likewise Parliamentarians. Her Education was in the Country; and her Father dying when she was but three Years of Age; and her Mother not living till she was twelve, what Improvements she has made, have been meerly by her own Industry and Application. She was married before the Age of Fifteen, to a Nephew of Sir *Stephen Fox*. This Gentleman living with her but a Year, she afterwards married Mr. *Carrol*, an Officer in the Army: And survived him likewise, in the space of a Year and half. She is since married to Mr. *Joseph Cent Livre*, Yeoman of the Mouth to his present Majesty. She was inclin'd to Poetry when very Young, having compos'd a Song before she was Seven Years old. She has wrote Fifteen Plays; her Talent is Comedy, particularly in the Contrivance of the Plots and Incidents; the Conduct and Beauty of which, are sufficiently recommended by Sir *Richard Steele*, in one of the *Spectator's*.

2. From [John Mottley], "Mrs. Susanna Centlivre," in "A Compleat List of All the English Dramatic Poets, and of All the Plays Ever Printed in the English Language, to the Present Year MDCCXLVII," appended to *Scanderbeg,* by Thomas Whincop (London: 1747) 185-188.

This Gentlewoman was the Daughter of one Mr. *Freeman* of *Holbeach* in *Lincolnshire*; and if we may give Credit to some private Stories concerning her, she had for a short Time a kind of University Education: for her own Mother, who was a Gentlewoman of a good Family, dying when she was a Child, and her Father marrying again, she was so ill-treated by her Mother-in-Law, when her Father was dead also, that she determined to come to *London*, with very little Money in her Purse, and almost destitute of every Necessary of Life, to seek a better Fortune than she was likely to obtain at home under a cruel Stepdame.

She had not travelled many Miles, but fatigued with her Journey and filled with a thousand perplexing Thoughts, she sat her down, with Tears in her Eyes, on a Bank by the Side of the Road, bewailing her lamentable Condition, when a young Gentleman from the University of *Cambridge,* [*Anthony Hammond,* Esq;] afterwards well known in the Polite and Literary World, chancing to come that Way, could not but take Notice of our weeping Damsel, then in the Bloom of Youth and Beauty, not quite fifteen Years of age, her Charms not diminished but rather heightened by her Tears: having enquired into the Cause of her Distress, he was so much moved with her Story, and the simple and affecting manner in which she related it, and more especially with her lovely Shape and Features, that he found himself so attached to her Person and Interest, that he could not think of parting with her, and of suffering her to pursue her painful Journey in the Condition she was in; he therefore intreated her to put herself under his Protection, which after some modest but faint Reluctance she consented to. He carried her to a Village not far from the University, where providing her with a Suit of Boys Clothes, he afterwards introduced her privately into the College, and his Intimates were told she was a Relation, whom he called by the Name of Cousin *Jack,* who was come to see him and the University, and pass a few Days there.

Jack was a smart little Fellow, learnt to fence, and, because the young Rogue had a Mind to be a Man before his Time, when the

Barber shaved his Cousin, he must perform his Office likewise on him; not that *Jack* had a Beard, but he wanted one. And that he might go away from College with a little more Learning than he brought thither, which is more than every one can say, his Cousin took a good deal of Pains to teach him a little Grammar. He instructed him also in some of the Terms of Logic, Rhetoric, and Ethics. As to *Metaphysics*, as *Hudibras* has it, he

> *Learnt* What's what, *and that's as high*
> As Metaphysic Wit *can fly.*

Jack, mightily pleased with his Cousin, and his Cousin with him, they passed some Months very agreeably together; but whether their Affair began to be smoked in College, or the Squire made that a Pretence only to get rid of a Companion he had had long enough to grow weary of, he told *Jack* one Morning that he was afraid they were watched a little more narrowly than he imagined, and that therefore for both their Reputations, he must think of leaving the University, but it should be for his Advantage; that he should go back to the Village where he had put on his Breeches, and resume the Sex he laid aside; that he would buy some things necessary, and send him to *London*, where he would recommend him to a Person, who should take care of him till he could follow, which should be with all the speed that his Affairs would allow of, and that he need not doubt but he would post after with the Wings of Love: Though in the mean Time, he should half break his Heart for the Loss of his Company.

The Young Lady, for she's *Jack* no longer, had no right to dispute his Commands, but consented to obey them, tho' with a heavy Heart; but her Misfortune was somewhat alleviated by the Hopes of seeing *London*; and by a very handsome Present he made her in Gold, and a Letter of Recommendation he gave her to a Gentlewoman of his Acquaintance, to treat her as the Daughter of a deceased Gentleman his Friend. Their Sighs and Tears at parting, their tender Sentiments of Love and Grief, I leave to the Reader's Imagination; and indeed they are better to be conceived than expressed.

Miss being arrived at *London*, pretty tolerably equipt, with some Money in her Pocket, and having the Assistance of an obliging good-natured Woman, who was willing to shew her all the Diversions of the Town, made her every Day less and less regret the Loss of her University Friend; and indeed she saw him not in many Years after....

The young Lady, in the mean Time, did not languish for an absent Lover. From her first coming to *London*, she took care to improve both the Charms of her Person and her Genius; she learnt *French*, and read a great deal of Poetry especially, but studied Men as well as Books.

The Play-house was the Meridian she chose to shine in, and it was impossible for her to appear often there without being taken Notice of and drawing many Admirers after her; but one Mr. *Fox*, a Nephew of the late Sir *Stephen Fox*, was the Person who bore her off in Triumph from a Cloud of Rivals. To this Gentleman she was married, or something like it; in the sixteenth Year of her Age; but, whether by Death, or whatever Accident it happened, they lived not together above one Year. He was succeeded in her Affections by one Mr. *Carrol*, a young Gentleman in the Army, who had the Misfortune to be killed in a Duel, about a Year and a half after his Marriage. This was a sensible Affliction to her. To divert her Melancholy, and partly perhaps for a Support, she now almost entirely devoted herself to the Muses, and it was under the name of *Carrol* that some of her first plays were published. Particularly *Love at a Venture*, a Comedy, which she offered to *Drury-lane* Theatre, where it was rejected, but she afterwards carried it to *Bath*, and there it was performed, and she herself acted a Part in it. Entered in the strolling Company, she attended them to several Parts of *England*, and about the Year 1706, the Court being at *Windsor*, she there put on her Breeches again, and acted the Part of ALEXANDER the GREAT, in the Tragedy of that Name. She played this Part, it seems, to great Perfection. How much she was admired by the rest of the Court is, at this Time, uncertain; but she so greatly charmed one Courtier, of inferior Rank indeed, Mr. *Joseph Centlivre*, one of her Majesty's Cooks, that he fell in Love with, and married her. With this Husband she lived the remaining Part of her Days, leaving him a Widower in the Year 1723. She dy'd at his House in *Spring-Garden* near *Charing-Cross* on the first of *December*, in the Year aforesaid, and was buried at *St. Martin's in the Fields*.

Mrs. *Centlivre* kept for many Years a constant Correspondence with a great Number of Gentlemen of Eminence and Wit, particularly, Sir *Richard Steele*, Mr. *Rowe*, Mr. *Budgell*, Dr. *Sewel*, Mr. *Amhurst*, &c.

If she had not a great deal of Wit in her Conversation, she had much Vivacity and good Humour; she was remarkably good-natured and benevolent in her Temper, and ready to do any friendly Office as far as was in her Power. She made herself some Friends and many Enemies by her strict Attachment to Whig Principles even in the most dangerous Times, and had she been a Man, I dare say would have freely ventured her Life in that Cause.

She lived in a decent clean Manner, and could shew (which I believe few other Poets could, who depended chiefly on their Pen) a great many Jewels and Pieces of Plate, which were the Produce of her own Labour, either purchased by the Money brought in by her Copies, her Benefit-Plays, or were Presents from Patrons. She had wrote before she dy'd no less than eighteen Dramatic Pieces, some of which are frequently acted, with Applause.

B: Criticism

3. From Elizabeth Inchbald, "Remarks" on *A Bold Stroke for a Wife*, *The British Theatre*, 11 (London, 1808):3-5.

Susannah Centlivre, the writer of this play, says of it, in her Dedication to the Duke of Wharton:—

> "All that I have to assert in favour of this piece is, that the plot is entirely new, and the incidents wholly owing to my own invention; not borrowed from our own, or translated from the works of any foreign poet; so that they have at least the charm of novelty to recommend them."

It would at present be more honourable to the authoress, that a reader should believe she had inconsiderately adopted the scenes of another, in the following play, than invented them herself. Still, in that supposition, much blame would attach to her taste and morality for the choice she had made in the adoption.

It is deeply to be lamented, that, at the time the most ingenious and witty of the English dramatists lived, there was no restraint, as at this period, upon the immorality of the stage. Plays would have come down to the present age, under such restrictions, less brilliant in humour and repartee, with fewer eulogiums from the admirers of wit;

but with fewer reproaches from the wise and the good, upon the evil tendency of the dramatic art.

The happy effect of the moral dramas of this aera, in impressing those persons with just sentiments who attend no other place of instruction but a theatre, has not yet erased from the mind of the prejudiced former ill consequences, from former plays.

Mrs. Centlivre, as a woman, falls more particularly under censure than her cotemporary writers:—though her temptations, to please the degraded taste of the public, were certainly more vehement than those of the authors, who wrote at that time; for they were men whose fortunes were not wholly dependent on their mental exertions; yet, the virtue of fortitude is expected from a female, when delicacy is the object which tries it; and the authoress of this comedy should have laid down her pen, and taken, in exchange, the meanest implement of labour, rather than have imitated the licentious example given her by the renowned poets of those days.

That Mrs. Centlivre was unfortunate from her birth, an orphan in her tender years, and a friendless wanderer at that age when most she required protection, has been already related in the sketch of her life affixed to her comedy of the "Busy Body:" the difficulties under which she had to struggle for subsistence, may plead some excuse to the indulgent, for her having in this one production, out of those which now keep a place upon the stage, applied to that disgraceful support of her Muse, to which her own sex of those times did not blush to attend as auditors. Nor can her offence be treated with excessive rigour in reference to the present time by those, who consider, that this very play of "A Bold Stroke for a Wife," is now frequently performed to an elegant, yet applauding audience.

The authoress has displayed high dramatic talents in the conception and execution of the various characters and incidents with which this play abounds. Herein the genius of Mrs. Centlivre consisted—the dialogue of her dramas might be given by a common writer, but her fable and events are proofs of a very extraordinary capacity.

But, in this comedy, however fertile her imagination has been in forming a multiplicity of occurrences, and diversifying the whole exhibition by variety of character, probability is so often violated, that the effect, though powerful, is that of farce, and not genuine comedy.

4. From Richard Cumberland, "Life of Susannah Centlivre", prefaced to *The Comedy of the Busy Body*, *The British Drama* (London, 1817), 10: n. pg.

As a writer, it is no very easy task to estimate her rank. It must be allowed that her plays do not abound with wit, and that the language of them is sometimes poor, enervate, incorrect, and puerile; but then her plots are busy and well-conducted, and her characters in general natural and well marked. But as plot and character are undoubtedly the soul of comedy; and language and wit, at best, but the clothing and external ornaments, it is certainly less excusable to shew a deficiency in the former than in the latter. And the success of some of Mrs. Centlivre's plays, plainly evince, that the first will strike the minds of the audience more powerfully than the last.... I have been confidently assured, that...[Robert Wilks] made use of this remarkable expression with regard to her *Bold Stroke for a Wife*, viz. *that not only her play would be damned, but she herself be damned for writing it.* Yet we find it still standing on the list of acting plays, nor is it ever performed without meeting with the approbation of the audience....

That Mrs. Centlivre was very perfectly acquainted with life, and closely read in the manners of mankind, no one, I think, can doubt who reads her comedies; but what appears to me the most extraordinary is, when we consider her history, the disadvantages she must have laboured under by being so early left to provide for herself, and that all the education she could have had must have been owing to her own application and assiduity; when we consider her as a self-cultivated genius, it is astonishing to find the traces of so much reading and learning as we meet with in many of her pieces. From the delineations of the various characters she has presented us with, she must have perfectly well understood the French, Dutch, and Spanish languages, besides the provincial dialects of her own. In a word, I cannot help giving it as my opinion, that if we do not allow her to be the very first of our female writers, she has but one above her, and may justly be placed next to her predecessor in dramatic glory, the great Mrs. Behn.

5. From Richard Cumberland, "Critique on the *Bold Stroke for a Wife*", *The British Drama* (London, 1817) 10: v-vii (of *A Bold Stroke*).

Why this play, with not one property to recommend it, but the harlequinade of the plot, and a most deterring penury of language, has been kept alive to this day, and may live for a hundred years to come, if times and taste do not alter, is easily understood. The versatility and adroitness of any one favourite actor, who can hit off the changeable character of Fainwell, will ensure success, so long as mimicry can charm the crowd.

....

In the second act Fainwell secures the vote and interest of Sir Philip Modelove, under the counterfeited appearance of a Frenchified fop.... The author...compensates in a great degree for the flatness of this dialogue, by the liveliness of the scene that concludes the act, in which the several guardians meet at Obadiah Prim's house, upon the summons of Sir Philip Modelove, who introduces Fainwell as a suitor whom he patronizes. The contempt with which the virtuoso Periwinkle, the merchant Tradelove, and the Quaker Prim, alternately declare their disapprobation of Fainwell, is well-marked, and managed with considerable spirit and address. For the conduct and contrivance of this interview Mrs. Centlivre is entitled to no little share of credit.

....

...Obadiah Prim and his spouse, with the humours of Simon Pure, contribute to form an intrigue, without question the most amusing of all, which Fainwell sets on foot for the attainment of his object; and of course this last transformation of our whimsical Proteus is judiciously reserved to form the climax of the plot, and to conclude the play. There is ingenuity in the arrangement and contrivance of a scene, that assembles so many persons on the stage at the same time with so great a contrariety of character. It is also an observation much to the credit of the poetess, and which for that reason I state with satisfaction, that, contrary to the case of very many comedies of higher pretensions, this of Mrs. Centlivre's is completely wound up with the fullest and most satisfactory attention to the close of every character that has been concerned in the business of it; and it cannot fail to strike the critical reader, how much more natural the acquiesence of the guardians is made to appear by the triumph which every one successively furnishes to the rest, when he makes discovery of the trick by which he has been duped.

C: Stockjobbing

6. From Daniel Defoe, *The Anatomy of Exchange Alley; or, A System of Stock-Jobbing: Proving that Scandalous Trade, As It Is Now Carried On, To Be Knavish in Its Private Practice, and Treason in Its Public* (London: 1719); rpt. John Francis, *Chronicles and Characters of the Stock Exchange* (Boston: 1850) 135-139, 148-150.

The general cry against stock-jobbing has been such, and people have been so long and so justly complaining of it as a public nuisance, and, which is still worse, have complained so long without a remedy, that the jobbers, hardened in crime, are at last come to exceed all bounds, and now, if ever, sleeping justice will awake, and take some notice of them, and if it should not now, yet the diligent creatures are so steady to themselves, that they will, some time or other, make it absolutely necessary to the government to demolish them.

I know they upon all occasions laugh at the suggestion, and have the pride to think it impracticable to restrain them; and one of the top of the function the other day, when I casually told him that, if they went on, they would make it absolutely necessary to the legislature to suppress them, returned, that he believed it was absolutely necessary for them to do it now as ever it could be. But how will they do it? It is impossible, said he; but if the government takes credit, their funds should come to market; and while there is a market, we will buy and sell. There is no effectual way in the world, says he, to suppress us but this, viz., that the government should first pay all the public debts, redeem all the funds, and dissolve all the charters, viz. Bank, South Sea, and East India, and buy nothing upon trust, and then, indeed, says he, they need not hang the stock-jobbers, for they will be apt to hang themselves.

I must confess, I in part agree that this is an effectual way; but I am far from thinking it the only way to deal with a consideration of usurers, who, having sold the whole nation to usury, keep the purse-strings of poor and rich in their hands, which they open and shut as they please.

But before I come to the needful ways for restraining those people, I think it will be of some service to expose their practices to common view, that the people may see a little what kind of dealers they are.

And first, they have this peculiar to them, and in which they outdo all the particular pieces of public knavery that ever I met with in the world, viz., that they have nothing to say for it themselves; they have, indeed, a particular stock of hardware, as the braziers call it, in their faces, to bear them out in it; but if you talk to them of their occupation, there is not a man but will own it is a complete system of knavery; that it is a trade founded in fraud, born of deceit, and nourished by trick, cheat, wheedle, forgeries, falsehoods, and all sorts of delusions; coining false news, this way good, that way bad; whispering imaginary terrors, frights, hopes, expectations, and then preying upon the weakness of those whose imaginations they have wrought upon, whom they have either elevated or depressed. If they meet with a cull, a young dealer that has money to lay out, they catch him at the door, whisper to him, "Sir, here is a great piece of news, it is not yet public, it is worth a thousand guineas but to mention it; I am heartily glad I met you, but it must be as secret as the black side of your soul, for they know nothing of it yet in the coffee-house; if they should, stock would rise ten per cent. in a moment, and I warrant you South Sea will be 130 in a week's time after it is known." "Well," says the weak creature, "pr'ythee, dear Tom, what is it?" "Well, really, Sir, I will let you into the secret, upon your honor to keep it till you hear it from other hands; why, it is this,—the Pretender is certainly taken, and is carried prisoner to the castle of Milan; there they have him fast. I assure you, the government had an express of it from my Lord St——s, within this hour." "Are you sure of it?" says the fish, who jumps eagerly into the net. "Sure of it! why, if you take your coach and go up to the secretaries' office, you may be satisfied of it yourself, and be down again in two hours, and, in the mean time, I will be doing something, though it is but little, till you return."

Away goes the gudgeon with his head full of wildfire, and a squib in his brain, and, coming to the place, meets a croney at the door, who ignorantly confirms the report, and so sets fire to the mine; for, indeed, the cheat came too far to be balked at home; so that, without giving himself time to consider, he hurries back full of the delusions, dreaming of nothing but of getting a hundred thousand pounds, or purchase two; and even this money was to be gotten only upon the views of his being beforehand with other people.

In this elevation he meets his broker, who throws more fireworks into the mine, and blows him up to so fierce an inflammation, that he employs him instantly to take guineas to accept stock of any kind, and almost at any price; for the news being now public, the artist made their price upon him. In a word, having accepted them for fifty thousand pounds more than he is able to pay, the jobber has got an estate, the broker two or three hundred guineas, and the esquire remains at leisure to sell his coach and horses, his fine seat and rich furniture, to make good the deficiency of his bear-skins; and, at last, when all will not go through it, he must give them a brush for the rest.

....

But now that I make good the charge, viz., that the whole art and mystery is a mere original system of cheat and delusion, I must let you see, too, that this part of the comedy may be very well called, "A Bite for the Biter," for which I must go back to the broker and his gudgeon; the moneyed gentleman finding himself let into the secret, indeed, and that he was bitten to the tune of £300,000 worse than nothing. After he had, unhappily, paid as far as his ready money would go, of which piece of honesty they say he has heartily repented, and is in hopes all that come after him will forgive him for the sake of what followed, stopped short, as he might well, you'll say, when his money was all gone, and bethinks himself, What am I doing! I have paid away all this money like a fool; I was drawn in like an ass, by the eager desire of biting my neighbours to a vast sum, and I have been fool enough in that; but I have been ten thousand times a worse fool to pay a groat of the money, especially since I knew I could not pay it all. Besides, who but I would have forgot the nature of the thing I was dealing in, and of the people I was dealing with? Why, is it not all a mere body of knavery? Is not the whole system of stock-jobbing a science of fraud? and are not all the dealers original thieves and pickpockets? Nay, do they not own it themselves? Have I not heard T.W., B.O., and F.S., a thousand times say they know their employment was a branch of highway robbing, and only differed in two things; first, in degree, viz., that it was ten thousand times worse, more remorseless, more void of humanity, done without necessity, and committed upon fathers, brothers, widows, orphans, and intimate friends; in all which cases, highwaymen, generally touched with remorse, and affected with principles of humanity and generosity, stopped short, and chose to prey upon strangers only.

Secondly, in danger, viz., that these rob securely; the other, with the utmost risk that the highwayman run, at the hazard of their lives, being sure to be hanged first or last, whereas these rob only at the hazard of their reputation, which is generally lost before they begin, and of their souls, which trifle is not worth the mentioning. Have not I, I say, heard my broker, Mr.——, say all this and much more, "That no man was obliged to make good any of their Exchange Alley bargains, unless he pleased, and unless he was in haste to part with his money, which, indeed, I am not; and have not all the brokers and jobbers, when they have been bitten too hard, said the same thing, and refused to pay?

....

"In a word, they are all a gang of rogues and cheats, and I'll pay none of them. Besides, my lawyer, Sir Thomas Subtle, tells me there is not a man of them dares sue me; *no, though I had no protection to fly to;* and he states the case thus:—

" 'You have, Sir,' says Subtle, 'contracted to accept of stock at a high price; East India at 220, Bank at 160, South Sea 120, and the like. Very well. They come to put it upon you, the stock being since fallen. Tell them you cannot take it yet; if they urge your contract, and demand when you will take it, tell them you will take it when you think fit.

" 'If they swagger, call names,—as rogue, cheat, and the like,— tell them, as to that, you are all of a fraternity; there is no great matter in it whether you cheat them, or they cheat you; 't is as it happens in the way of trade; that it all belongs to the craft; and, as the Devil's broker, Whiston, said to parson Giffard, tell them you are all of a trade. If they rage, and tell you the Devil will have you, and such as that, tell them they should let the Devil and you alone to agree about that, it is none of their business; but when he comes for you, tell them you would advise them to keep out of the way, or get a protection, as you have against them.

" 'After this, it is supposed they will sue you at law. Then leave it to me; I'll hang them up for a year or two in our courts; and if ever in that time the stock comes up to the price, we will tender the money in court, demand the stock, and saddle the charges of the suit upon them. Let them avoid it if they can.'

"This is my lawyer's opinion," says he to himself, "and I'll follow it to a tittle; and so we are told he has; and I do not hear that one stock-jobber has begun to sue him yet, or intends it; nor, indeed, dare they do it."

This experiment, indeed, may teach understanding to every honest man that falls into the clutches of these merciless men, called stock-jobbers; and I give the world this notice, that, in short, not one of their Exchange Alley bargains need be otherwise than thus complied with. And, let these buyers of bear-skins remember it, not a man of them dare go to common law to recover the conditions; nor is any man obliged, farther than he thinks himself obliged in principle, to make good one of his bargains with them. How far principle will carry any man to be just to a common cheat, that has drawn him into a snare, I do not, indeed, know; but I cannot suppose it will go a very great length, where there is so clear, so plain, and so legal a door to get out at.

....

[T]he Alley throngs with Jews, jobbers, and brokers; their names are needless, their characters dirty as their employment; and the best thing that I can yet find to say of them is, that there happens to be two honest men among them,—Heavens preserve their integrity; for the place is a snare, the employment itself fatal to principle, and hitherto, the same observation which I think was very aptly made upon the Mint, will justly turn upon them,—that many an honest man has gone in to them, but cannot say that I ever knew one come an honest man out from them.

But to leave them a little, and turn our eyes another way, is it not surprising to find new faces among these scandalous people, and persons even too big even for our reproof? Is it possible that stars of another latitude should appear in our hemisphere? Had it been Sims or Bowcher, or gamesters of the drawing-rooms or masquerades, there had been little to be said; or had the groom-porters been transposed to Garraway's and Jonathan's, it had been nothing new; true gamesters being always ready to turn their hand to any play. But to see statesmen turn dealers, and men of honor stoop to the chicanery of jobbing; to see men at the offices in the morning, at the P—- house about noon, at the cabinet at night, and at Exchange Alley in the proper intervals, what new phenomena are these? What fatal things may these shining planets (like the late great light) foretell to the state and to the public; for when statesmen turn jobbers, the state may be jobbed.

It may be true that a treasurer or cash-keeper may be trusted with more money than he is worth, and many times it is so; and if the man be honest, there may be no harm in it: but when a treasurer plays for more money then he is worth, they that trust him run a risk of their money, because, though he may an honest man, he may be undone. I speak of private, not public treasurers.

Indeed, it requires some apology to say such a one may be an honest man; it would be hard to call him an honest man, who plays away any man's money that is not his own. But if it be dishonest to play it away, that is, lose it at play, 't is equally dishonest to play with it, whether it be lost or no; because, in such a case, he that plays for more than he can pay, his master runs the hazard more than himself; nay, his master runs an unequal hazard, for if the money be lost, 't is the master's, if there is gain, 't is the servant's.

Stock-jobbing is play; a box and dice may be less dangerous, the nature of them are alike a hazard; and if they venture at either what is not their own, the knavery is the same. It is not necessary, any more than it is safe, to mention the persons I may think of in this remark; they who are the men will easily understand me.

In a word, I appeal to all the world, whether a man that is intrusted with other men's money (whether public or private is not the question) ought to be seen in Exchange Alley. Would it not be a sufficient objection to any gentleman or merchant, not to employ any man to keep his cash, or look after his estate, to say of him he plays, he is a gamester, or he is given to gaming and stock-jobbing, which is still worse, gives the same, or a stronger ground of objection in like cases.

Again, are there fewer sharpers and setters in Exchange Alley than at the Groom Porters? Is there less cheating in stock-jobbing than at play? Or, rather, is there not fifty times more? An unentered youth coming to deal in Exchange Alley is immediately surrounded with bites, setters, pointers, and the worst set of cheats, just as a young country gentleman is with bawds, pimps, and spongers, when he first comes to town. It is ten thousand to one, when a forward young tradesman steps out of his shop into Exchange Alley, I say 't is ten thousand to one but he is undone: if you see him once but enter the fatal door, never discount his bills afterwards, never trust him with goods at six months' pay any more.

If it be thus dangerous to the mean, what is it to the great? I see only this difference, that in the first the danger is private, in the latter public.